VIDEOCONFERENCING FOR SCHOOLS: PEDAGOGY AND PRACTICE

Marie Martin, Ed.D

To Larry
With every good wish
Marie Martin

D1248161

First published in May 2008

Guildhall Press
Ráth Mór Business Park
Bligh's Lane
Derry, N Ireland, BT48 0LZ
T: (028) 7136 4413 F: (028) 7137 2949
info@ghpress.com www.ghpress.com

ABOUT THE AUTHOR

A former teacher of Modern Languages and former International Officer with the Western Education & Library Board, Marie Martin is one of the pioneers of the use of videoconferencing in education in Northern Ireland. In 2007, she gained a doctorate in education, specialising in education technology, from Duquesne University, Pittsburgh, USA. She currently teaches as adjunct faculty at two US universities, using distance education technologies, including videoconferencing, to deliver courses. She also advises C2k on aspects of videoconferencing. She has published extensively on this technology and has presented at education conferences in the UK, Ireland, the USA and South America.

FOREWORD

I have great pleasure in welcoming you to Marie Martin's much-anticipated book *Videoconferencing for Schools: Pedagogy and Practice*. The book explores the extensive range of videoconferencing activities which have taken place in schools across Northern Ireland. There are twenty-eight case studies which illustrate how videoconferencing can have a powerful effect on learning and teaching. They describe many examples of successful videoconferencing activities, from the enabling of interactive and flexible workshops for continuing professional development, through inter-school collaboration locally and globally, to the setting up of virtual visits and field trips – all contributing to the enrichment and extension of the curriculum.

In addition to exploring professional development and curriculum applications of videoconferencing, the book provides valuable practical advice on best-practice videoconferencing in the classroom. It offers a rich resource of advice from planning the videoconferencing session, through videoconferencing etiquette to evaluating the videoconferencing session.

Over the past decade, Marie Martin has worked tirelessly to promote the creative use of videoconferencing in schools in Northern Ireland and beyond; this book contains her diverse experience and knowledge. Not only is it a compendium of knowledge, but it also showcases the innovative videoconferencing work that is being undertaken in Northern Ireland's schools.

This is a book that will benefit all teachers, no matter where they are, who are interested in starting to use, or who want to integrate, videoconferencing into the classroom. It will motivate and provide confidence. I warmly recommended it to everyone concerned with the future of education.

Jimmy Stewart
Director, C2k

TABLE OF CONTENTS

PREFACE

Videoconferencing may well be a technology whose time in education has come. Until recently, for a number of reasons, including cost, connectivity issues and the perceived technical unreliability of the medium, its use in education – other than at university level – has been relatively limited. However, reduction in costs, advances in technology, increased bandwidth and the emergence of the virtually cost-free and increasingly reliable IP connectivity now make this unique, real-time, interactive audiovisual medium more attractive to schools. I have been encouraged by Classroom 2000 (C2k) to write this book to help meet the needs of schools interested in using videoconferencing or in extending their use of it. It is based on my own experience and that of other educators in the field in Northern Ireland from the mid-1990s to the present.

The 2004 Report on Videoconferencing in the Classroom for the Department for Education and Skills (England and Wales) makes a useful distinction between effective videoconferencing and successful videoconferencing. In broad terms, effective videoconferencing is when good learning takes place. Successful videoconferencing is when the technology works well and when due attention has been paid to the logistics relating to using videoconferencing for a learning event. The two are, of course, interrelated, but each requires its own approaches and strategies. The structure of this book reflects these requirements. It is in two parts. The first part describes the unique capabilities of videoconferencing technology (Chapter One), suggests how these can be exploited to make good learning happen (Chapter Two), and provides examples of good practice from schools across Northern Ireland (Chapter Three). The second part offers detailed practical guidance on setting up, organising and implementing a videoconference (Chapter Four). The appendices provide information on print and electronic resources, including links to content providers, for those wishing to explore further (Appendix A), a sample matrix and lesson plans (Appendix B), an evaluation template (Appendix C), a glossary (Appendix D), and information on the C2k managed videoconferencing service (Appendix E).

In the past decade in Northern Ireland, those of us interested in exploring the potential of videoconferencing to enrich and extend learning have necessarily adopted a learning-by-doing approach. This book shares what many of us have learned. My hope is that it will encourage others to learn by doing, and that what is shared in these pages will help make the learning curve easy, enriching and enjoyable.

Acknowledgements

I would like to express my gratitude to the teachers who shared with me the videoconferencing stories that make up the Good Practice section of this book. My thanks are also due to Carol McAlister, Louise Heaney and Jayne McIlgorm of C2k for their unfailing support and guidance, to the members of the C2k Videoconferencing Group for their interest and encouragement, to Peter Simpson of the North-Eastern Education and Library Board (NEELB) for his generous sharing of his experience and expertise, and to my former colleagues in the Western Education and Library Board (WELB) who, over a period of almost ten years, facilitated my exploration of the potential of videoconferencing to enrich and extend the learning experience in schools.

CHAPTER ONE:
Videoconferencing and its Application in Education

What is videoconferencing?

Videoconferencing is basically interactive television. It allows people in different locations anywhere in the world to see and talk to one another and to share applications and resources in real time. It is a flexible technology which can link participants in two or more locations. It can be used for a wide variety of educational purposes, both curricular and administrative, and by a wide variety of group sizes. It is user-friendly and requires little or no technical knowledge for normal use in teaching and learning.

Why use videoconferencing?

In general terms, videoconferencing can be used to help overcome the barriers to face-to-face communication that are imposed by distance, time, expense and the limitations of human energy. It does this by replicating such communication virtually and in real time. In addition, in the ecological context, videoconferencing can reduce our carbon foot print.

Its potential uses in education are wide-ranging. They all involve the movement of information rather than people. In this book, they are summarised under four main headings:

- ▶ Curriculum extension – accessing or delivering subject specific classes not available within a single school;
- ▶ Curriculum enrichment – bringing the outside world into the classroom through interactive, audiovisual, real-time learning experiences;
- ▶ Inter-school collaborative work, both locally and globally;
- ▶ Professional development – teachers accessing early and continuous development through distance learning courses and through networking with colleagues in other schools.

In addition, videoconferencing can support the development of many so-called "soft" skills that are increasingly relevant to the 21st century workplace and are also central to the revised Northern Ireland curriculum. Employers now make clear that, while "hard" qualifications are important, they are no longer enough. They are looking, in addition, for employees with self-confidence, good communication and presentation skills, team-working and problem-solving skills, creative and innovative thinking, and the ability to engage in lifelong learning. Videoconferencing can foster the development of these skills, as well as helping to meet the needs of the new generation of digital learners who have grown up in a technology-saturated society that has shaped their attitude to learning and their learning styles.

The good practice examples in Chapter Three will demonstrate how videoconferencing can be used to help deliver both hard outcomes and soft skills. Specifically, it can be used to:

- ▶ set up authentic beyond-the-school learning situations;
- ▶ connect learners to experts, other communities and other experiences;
- ▶ promote multi-school project collaboration;
- ▶ encourage pupils to be active rather than passive learners;
- ▶ facilitate access to primary sources of information;
- ▶ promote problem-solving skills;
- ▶ foster higher order thinking skills;
- ▶ accommodate learners of all ages and abilities:
- ▶ appeal to a variety of learning styles;
- ▶ improve social skills, including the ability to work with others;
- ▶ improve communication and presentation skills;
- ▶ enhance the motivation of pupils and teachers;
- ▶ improve the self-esteem and self-confidence of pupils;
- ▶ promote the enjoyment of learning;
- ▶ raise the awareness and appreciation of cultural diversity;
- ▶ raise the awareness and appreciation of citizenship issues and responsibilities;
- ▶ promote educational and social inclusion.

These outcomes are, of course, not achieved automatically. They are attained through effective teaching and learning strategies. How to make good learning happen when using videoconferencing is the focus of the next chapter.

CHAPTER TWO:
A Pedagogy for Effective Videoconferencing

Making good learning happen with videoconferencing

In the virtual world, as in the traditional classroom, good teaching matters. Studies have shown that a good classroom teacher is usually a good teacher when using videoconferencing. Good teachers are never content with simply transferring knowledge to passive pupils. They devise strategies to encourage pupils to be active, independent learners and to enjoy the learning process. Videoconferencing supports this approach. Good teaching and learning strategies for videoconferencing are also effective strategies for the traditional face-to-face learning situation. In short, using videoconferencing effectively in teaching and learning has less to do with the technology itself than with the teacher's attitude to it and the way the teacher uses it.

Uniquely, videoconferencing enables participants to come together face-to-face virtually and in real time. Because of this capability, it comes closest to replicating the traditional classroom, while greatly enriching and extending the curriculum by authentic, beyond-the-classroom learning experiences. However, this enrichment does not happen automatically. The elements of distance and of physical separation of teacher and pupils and – in the case of collaborative work – of pupils from one another must be given careful consideration when designing a learning experience by videoconferencing. An additional issue is that this technology can carry the baggage of passive viewing associated with other visual media such as film and television. The challenge is to keep the geographically separated participants actively engaged with one another and with the learning process.

Videoconferencing functions best when understood as a technology for learning rather than for teaching and when used in the context of an interactive, pupil-centred pedagogy. Careful planning and preparation are essential to ensure this approach. Gaining awareness of the particular characteristics of videoconferencing, particularly its real-time interactive capability, is a necessary preliminary step to ensure fitness for purpose and to maximise the potential of the technology. Learners' needs should always drive the technology. Learning goals, aligned with the curriculum and deliverable by videoconferencing, should be set first. The videoconferencing element should be integrated into the overall lesson or unit, the aim being to broaden and deepen pupils' understanding of the topic being studied and to widen their horizons.

Interaction is essential to effective learning in this environment, whether videoconferencing is being used for teaching or for peer collaboration. Relationships always matter in the learning experience, possibly more so in the virtual than in the real classroom where physical presence helps to sustain them. Technology is sometimes perceived as a dehumanising factor in learning. However, designing strategies for real time interaction can counteract this, by fostering relationships and keeping the vital human element to the fore in the virtual learning experience. In this way, technology can be used to deliver learning that nourishes the human spirit. Videoconferencing is uniquely placed to support this learning goal. Evaluation, therefore, should focus not only on the "hard benefits" of learning outcomes and pupil performance, but also on the "soft benefits" such as real life relevance, quality and range of the learning experience, motivation, and enjoyment of the learning process leading to a love of learning.

Strategies need to be devised to facilitate a high level of interaction between the teacher and pupils, between the pupils themselves, between the pupils and the lesson content and learning materials, and between the learners and the videoconferencing technology. The shift must be from passive to active and interactive. Strategies for interaction during the videoconference should be designed and constantly fostered by the teacher. Some suggested strategies are set out below.

Strategies for interaction

Strategies for interaction could include:

▶ designing for social interaction at the start of the videoconference and for fostering a sense of social presence throughout the videoconference. This helps to promote a good relationship between teacher and pupils when a class is accessing a distance lesson. In collaborative learning situations, social interaction between pupils also helps them to forget about the technology and to create a feeling of "almost being there", of "dealing with real people". This in turn helps to reduce the potential stress of being "on camera" and is highly effective in enabling pupils to work in a relaxed but alert manner that is conducive to learning and to enjoyment of the learning process. This was highlighted in the comment of a pupil who had just participated by videoconferencing in a distance learning class: "That was great fun! It brought learning to life! I totally forgot about the technology."

▶ designing a range of interactive learning activities to involve pupils early and often. The importance of this cannot be overstated, given not only the inherent capabilities of videoconferencing, but also the characteristics of today's digital generation of learners. Much informal learning has always taken place outside school hours. In their after-school life, today's young people are saturated with interactive "fun" technologies such as multi-player games, and they immerse themselves in social Internet activities such as wikis, blogs, and social networking sites. In all of these, they experience informal learning as a challenging, meaning-making social activity that engages their emotions as well as their minds. Videoconferencing can support this "hard fun" approach in the formal learning situation.

▶ designing for pace and variety. Keep the "talking head" syndrome to a minimum. Where the learning experience cannot be interactive, keep to the "10-15-minute segment" rule for content input. Aim for "nuggets of information". Design to involve pupils again after each segment in ways that appeal to a range of intelligences and learning styles, e.g. questions and discussions for the aural and interpersonal learners; student presentations, graphics, video clips for visual learners; role plays for kinaesthetic learners. Use peripheral technologies, such as document camera/visualiser, video player/DVD, data projector; PC for PowerPoint presentations, and the interactive whiteboard to add variety of delivery and to vary the pace of the learning event. Where appropriate, design for application sharing and the sharing of human resources, e.g. guest speakers.

▶ fostering dialogue between participants at different sites as a means of negotiating meaning. This can be immensely powerful and can lead to higher order thinking and to the honing of problem-solving skills.

▶ fostering a sense of community of learners among the geographically separated pupils by forming cross-site project groups and encouraging collaboration rather than competition.

▶ adapting the roles of teacher and pupils to benefit from the new learning environment. Given the short shelf-life of knowledge today, the teacher, whether physically present or at a distance, can only be part content provider and is called to focus on the more challenging role of facilitating learning – of making learning happen. With videoconferencing, a significant measure of autonomy can be given to learners. Learner scaffolding/support is, however, essential in order to build up self-confidence and set pupils up for success.

▶ ensuring that a facilitator or teacher is present at the remote/far site to provide scaffolding to the distant pupils and to encourage interactivity.

▶ ensuring agreement, when accessing a distant expert, on the need for an interactive approach. During the videoconference, the teacher could act as chair or facilitator to ensure that this approach is sustained.

Strategies for pupil scaffolding

Pupil scaffolding can be fostered before the videoconference through:

▶ involving pupils, where appropriate, in each stage of the preparation, including the content, their own input, setting up the room and operation of the technology – after they have received basic training in the latter;

▶ helping pupils develop the skill of framing relevant questions and sending these in advance when accessing a distant expert;

▶ providing opportunities for pupils to practise "on camera" presentation and communication skills;

▶ ensuring pupils understand videoconferencing etiquette (See Chapter 4);

▶ clarifying the changes in the role of teacher and pupils – teacher as learning facilitator, pupils as active, independent learners – and encouraging this approach in follow-on activities in the classroom;

- demonstrating enthusiasm for the technology – something which pupils quickly pick up on;
- setting expectations for interactivity;
- providing pupils with appropriate handouts and other support materials.

During the videoconference, scaffolding is provided by the teacher's careful chairing and monitoring of the experience, assisted by the remote site facilitator, to ensure adherence to the strategies designed for interaction among participants and active engagement in the learning process. More detailed guidelines for teaching by videoconference are set out in Chapter Two.

After the videoconference, scaffolding/support can take the form of:
- positive feedback to pupils on their performance;
- inviting immediate oral assessment from pupils;
- involving pupils as partners with the teacher, facilitator and technical support person – if this support is provided – in the assessment and evaluation of the videoconference;
- explaining to pupils, as appropriate to age and ability, the criteria to be used in overall evaluation;
- seeking written assessment of the videoconference from pupils, to include self-assessment of their performance and reactions as well as suggestions for improvement of the experience (See sample evaluation form in Appendix C);
- recording of the conference for evaluation and reinforcement;
- provision of opportunities to use the new knowledge and skills.

Obviously, the degree of scaffolding/support needed is greater when pupils are inexperienced in learning by videoconferencing. It can be gradually reduced – and pupil autonomy increased – as pupils become more familiar with the technology.

The case studies in Chapter Three will illustrate the effectiveness of these strategies in making good learning happen when using videoconferencing.

CHAPTER THREE:
Effective Videoconferencing – Good Practice in Schools

Case studies: Introduction

Although, to date, videoconferencing has been a relatively underused technology in schools, there exists a body of good practice in Northern Ireland dating back to the mid-1990s. Indeed, even earlier than that (1986), the ongoing European Studies project had introduced videoconferencing as well as other emerging collaborative technologies into its participating schools in Ireland and across Europe. In particular, since 1999, the cross-border Dissolving Boundaries project has done much in a sustained and structured way to highlight the role of the new technologies, including videoconferencing, in promoting quality learning in schools, and in fostering cultural awareness and mutual understanding through partnering schools throughout the island of Ireland and throughout Europe. Interestingly, in the reports on this project, videoconferencing has been frequently identified as the preferred technology of pupils at all levels but particularly in the special needs sector.

Yet, outside these two projects, as elsewhere – in the UK, Ireland and other countries – videoconferencing was largely undervalued, and good practice was confined to a few areas where "champions" began to build up experience and expertise in a learning- by-doing approach. Recently, however, in Northern Ireland, in the context of the revised curriculum and, in particular, of the curriculum entitlement framework, there are instances of the creative application of videoconferencing in primary and post-primary schools among recent adopters of the technology. The case studies in this section have been selected from the innovative work of these early champions and recent adopters. They will illustrate how teachers have exploited the unique real-time audiovisual capabilities of the technology in order to bring real-world, interactive learning experiences into the classroom (and other learning places) to all learners – including the teachers themselves. Although the case studies are presented thematically rather than chronologically, they will cover the period from the mid-1990s to the present day. For the early period, I will draw on some of my own experiences in exploring the potential of videoconferencing as International Officer with the WELB, as well as on that of others working in this field. For the later period, I will include ongoing projects and some recent and current examples of good practice from schools in different parts of Northern Ireland.

The case studies are not meant to be exhaustive. Those used here are intended to be a sample of the good work that has been done and is being done by creative teachers in Northern Ireland in using videoconferencing in the classroom. They demonstrate how videoconferencing, in the hands of such teachers, can create an enriched learning environment that is conducive to enhancing and extending the curriculum, as well as to fostering the "portable skills" of problem-solving, working in cross-cultural teams, critical thinking, and learning-to-learn, and the so-called "soft skills" of self-esteem and self-confidence, social and communication skills, all of which are now increasingly in demand in the constantly changing global market place of the 21st century. Past experience has shown that such authentic stories – based on work in local schools – can help encourage and motivate teachers who are unfamiliar with this technology, or who are seeking innovative ways of using it. Teachers like to hear it from teachers. This is their reality check. Attention is also drawn to the factors, identified by practitioners in the field, which made for an effective videoconference-mediated learning experience in terms of learning objectives and outcomes.

Case studies: Background

In the mid-1990s, very few schools had videoconferencing systems on their premises. The WELB therefore adopted the strategy of bringing pupils into the Board's Technology Education Centre – or one of its Teachers' Centres – and used the Board's facilities to link them with schools in other parts of the world. However, where possible, we also supported school-based videoconferencing. This included lending a basic videoconferencing system to schools for project-related communication, as well as working in schools to encourage teachers to use the school's own equipment, where such existed. This approach was also adopted by other Boards, e.g. the NEELB, which, through its Assistant Technology Advisor, Peter Simpson, is still responsible for much of the ongoing trail-blazing work in videoconferencing.

At a very early stage in our experiments with videoconferencing, we learned a significant lesson that is as valid now as it was then. We discovered that success depended less on the technology itself than on the creative and innovative teachers who agreed to join us in a learning-by–doing approach. Rich learning experiences were achieved using relatively unsophisticated technology – in our case, the basic, now obsolete, VC 7000. These experiences included accessing distance teaching and learning from external providers, access to experts, school collaboration across distance, virtual field trips and professional development. Some examples of good practice in these areas are set out in the case studies in this chapter. They illustrate the effective application of videoconferencing over a wide range of key stages, curriculum areas, learning styles and abilities. It is, perhaps, worth noting that the videoconferencing guidelines and etiquette sections offered in this book are the fruits of the learning curve that began for us in the mid-1990s and is still continuing.

The case studies are divided into five areas:
A. Curriculum extension
B. Curriculum enrichment
C. Collaborative distance learning
D. Professional development
E. The future

A. CURRICULUM EXTENSION: DISTANCE TEACHING AND LEARNING

Arising from the review of post-primary education, there is a need for collaboration among schools and with Further and Higher Education in order to extend the curriculum and to secure the full range of curriculum provision, both vocational and academic. In this context, it is useful to look at projects dating from the mid-1990s to the present day that explore the potential of videoconferencing to help extend the curriculum by enabling distance teaching and learning.

Case Study 1
Modern Languages: KS 4

In 1996, in partnership with the University of Ulster (UU) at Magee, the WELB engaged in its first distance teaching and learning project, providing a six-week curriculum extension module on Business French, taught from Magee, to two rural secondary schools (Castlederg High School and St. Eugene's High School, Castlederg). The objectives were to explore the potential of videoconferencing to extend the curriculum of small rural schools by providing a subject not offered on the school curriculum, to assess pupils' reaction to the distance learning experience and to learn, by doing, the strategies and techniques that enable good distance teaching. The Board supplied a basic videoconferencing system on loan to Castlederg High School, arranged for an ISDN line into the school and provided technical support. Joint distance classes, taught by a member of the Faculty of Humanities at the Magee campus of the University for pupils from both schools, were held on a weekly basis for a period of six weeks. The teacher at Magee and the pupils at the schools reacted very positively to the experience. Learning outcomes were assessed by the teacher from Magee and the classroom teacher as being satisfactory, and all stakeholders – the WELB, the UU at Magee and the schools – found that the pilot project showed the potential of videoconferencing, properly used, as a tool for delivering meaningful distance learning.

A number of success factors were identified in this early pilot project. These informed the Board's future initiatives in this field. The main factor was the importance of the distance teacher, illustrating what good teaching can achieve with even basic videoconferencing technology. Other factors included:

▶ careful preparation;

▶ establishing a good relationship between the teacher and pupils at an early stage – this was achieved by the teacher visiting the pupils in person prior to the beginning of the course;

▶ setting ground rules with the school for acceptable behaviour of pupils;

▶ having a facilitator (usually the classroom teachers, off-screen) at the distant site;

▶ adapting teaching strategies to suit the technology;

▶ providing pupils with support materials;

▶ giving clear instructions – including contact details – about follow-up work.

These factors were taken fully into account in a later distance learning project. This involved native French students, who were attending Magee College under the EU Erasmus programme, providing tutorials in oral French to pupils in rural secondary schools that did not have a language assistant. These same factors are also evident in recent distance learning projects in other parts of Northern Ireland.

Case Study 2
Geography and Biology: KS 4

A much more sophisticated distance teaching and learning experience took place in 1999 when Key Stage 4 pupils from Strabane Grammar School took part in a geography enhancement lesson delivered via videoconference from the Liberty Science Center, New Jersey, to the WELB's Technology Education Centre, Omagh. The learning objectives were to enhance the pupils' understanding of coastal erosion and to deepen their understanding of the differences between aquatic species and how they react with their habitat. These topics formed part of the geography and biology curricula. The lesson began with an outdoor virtual trip along the Hudson River Estuary, followed by an indoor interactive lesson. The content and format of the lesson had been agreed in advance by the Liberty Science Center and the subject teachers. Learning objectives were agreed, a lesson plan was drawn up and interactive strategies were devised to maximise the potential of videoconferencing. These involved a high degree of problem-solving through remotely directing alterations to a previously prepared model of the Hudson River Estuary on display in the distant classroom. A brief comparison was then made with Lough Foyle, with the Strabane pupils making a presentation of their study of the Foyle Estuary.

The pupils greatly enjoyed the virtual classroom experience, and were fully engaged throughout the lesson. One pupil described it as "a great way of bringing learning to life". The learning outcomes in terms of a deeper understanding of the topics were assessed as highly satisfactory by both the classroom teachers and the pupils. The latter found the experience of videoconference-mediated learning highly motivating. They responded enthusiastically to the interactive nature of the distant lesson. They were enthusiastic about the virtual trip element of the lesson, and about the challenge of the problem-solving activities and of communicating and presenting their own work. The teachers stated that it contributed to their professional development by exposing them to a new and powerful learning technology which contributed to their own knowledge and understanding, gave them an insight into the value of a more interactive teaching paradigm, and involved them in learning conversations with teaching colleagues from the other side of the world.

The main success factors were undoubtedly careful preparation, the virtual trip experience, the high level of interactivity, and using a variety of teaching strategies appropriate to the technology.

Case Study 3
Geography and Physics: Post-16

Following this success, Strabane Grammar School arranged for another distance lesson with the Liberty Science Center. This time the curriculum enhancement areas were A level Geography and Physics. Teachers from the two departments liaised by email with the Liberty Science Center to ensure that the distance lesson would be relevant to the A level curriculum. Again, an agreed lesson plan was drawn up, including the required preparations to be done by pupils in order to derive maximum benefits from the virtual lesson. This preparation included researching recommended websites and using worksheets provided by Liberty Science Center. The virtual lesson was highly interactive, involving "building your own earthquake" by remotely entering variables into the Center's "Earthquake Simulator". This proved to be a "hard fun" experience which the pupils loved. Once again, the teacher found that it not only extended the pupils' knowledge and understanding of the subject, but enhanced their problem-solving skills, and increased their motivation and their enjoyment of learning.

Case Study 4
Technology: Post-16

The following case study is a current example of how cross-phase distant teaching using videoconferencing can help schools extend their existing provision. In the academic year 2006-2007, St. Louis Grammar School, Kilkeel, successfully completed their first project of curriculum enrichment and extension through videoconferencing. In the context of the curriculum entitlement framework, they aimed to explore the viability of using video-conferencing to receive lessons from Newry College of Further and Higher Education. The objective was to teach a software programme called Solid Works to a group of Year 13 pupils as part of their technology course. This software is used mainly for 3D design graphics and is regarded as highly useful and beneficial for coursework. Videoconferencing was used to deliver the lessons covering the full range of required knowledge from basic elements to complex demands. The school used the new Virtual Classroom system. This is a desktop collaboration suite with audio and video conferencing, messaging and whiteboard capabilities. It operates using 'virtual rooms', which participants enter to join a session. A web-cam and audio devices (headset or external microphone and speakers) are used for audio and video conferencing. As well as videoconferencing, participants can show presentations to one another, share applications and create documents collaboratively. St. Louis pupils found the system easy to operate and received ongoing support from C2k who were piloting the system. In order to enable the whole group to participate in the lesson, the class teacher displayed the video output on the class whiteboard and used speakers to relay audio output. An external microphone was used for audio input from the St. Louis class. This allowed the pupils to control the pace of the lesson and to be active rather than passive participants.

On completion of the unit, the class teacher, who had had no previous experience of videoconferencing, was satisfied that the pupils had gained high level knowledge of the Solid Works programme. He attributed this first of all to the fact that the motivational potential of videoconferencing as a technology for learning had been exploited. His pupils responded well to the interactive strategies used by the distant teacher, were comfortable with the technology and greatly enjoyed this new way of learning. He also identified other success factors:

- ▶ devoting some time in advance to preparation, including timetabling, and setting up and testing the system to minimise the risk of technical problems getting in the way of the learning;
- ▶ prioritising a good audio system so that pupils could always hear and interact with the teacher. This meant that the lesson could be at a pupil-friendly pace and could avoid the "talking head" syndrome. (This is in line with research findings that audio is even more important than image for sustaining interest and ensuring interactive communication.)
- ▶ having the distant tutor meet the pupils in person in advance of the lessons to establish a good rapport and to make the experience more human.

The class teacher's overall reaction was that videoconferencing is a highly efficient resource, provided it is used correctly. He would strongly recommend it for teaching technology software such as Solid Works.

Case Study 5
Law: Post-16

St. Malachy's High School, Castlewellan, see videoconferencing as an important technology for extending the curriculum by enabling the delivery of a range of additional subjects. In the academic year 2006-2007, the school was able to purchase a one-year course in Law from an external professional distance learning course provider. The classes were delivered once a week using videoconferencing. From the experience, the class teacher found that a major factor for success was preparing pupils to be independent learners. Pupils who are normally more passive, dependent learners found the experience extremely demanding. Others welcomed the opportunity to take ownership of their learning. The teacher made the significant observation that pupils who succeed in meeting the challenge of learning in the virtual classroom are very well prepared for university and for the demands of the outside world. The externally provided Law course is being continued in the current academic year. The school has also purchased a distance learning course in French.

Case Study 6
Distant teaching for special needs: KS 1

To illustrate the versatility of videoconferencing in catering for individual pupils as well as for groups and its capability of including pupils of all ages and abilities in quality distance learning, I will cite an example of good practice relating to a seven year old pupil with special needs in a small primary school on an island off the south-west coast of Ireland. I observed a typical virtual lesson in the year 2000, while supporting the integration of videoconferencing in a group of rural schools in West Cork, as part of a project between that region and the WELB under the framework of a European network of rural schools. The island primary school had an enrolment of 19 pupils, one of whom had severe learning difficulties. Because of access problems to the island under poor weather conditions, this pupil could not receive the regular learning support from specialist teachers that was available on the mainland. The objective was to explore the potential of videoconferencing to facilitate virtual access. Funding was secured to install a videoconferencing system in the school. From another school in the network, which was on the mainland, a Learning Support teacher conducted weekly sessions by videoconference with the young pupil with severe learning difficulties. During the subsequent evaluation, the teacher expressed the opinion that certain sections of the programme, such as the use of camera close up when helping the pupil to link new letters to correct sounds, were probably more effective in the videoconference than in a traditional face-to-face lesson. The lesson which lasted 30 minutes was always sharply focused. The teacher stated that she felt she got more work done in a distant teaching and learning session than in an actual classroom situation where pupils could be easily distracted.

Several aspects of the lesson which I observed can be identified as success factors. A face-to-face meeting between the distant teacher and the pupil had taken place prior to the virtual lessons, when she went over to the island to assess him, and they had established a good rapport. The teacher adapted her methodology to exploit the benefits of the technology. The lesson was interactive and contained plenty of variety. The child's self-esteem was obviously greatly enhanced by the distance learning experience which he greatly enjoyed.

Some extracts from a tribute paid to the project managers by the school principal during a videoconference will give an idea of the impact of videoconferencing on the hitherto isolated island school. "Videoconferencing has transformed my life and that of my pupils. … I can see my colleagues on the mainland on a regular basis. Now, my pupils can see the children in other schools and take part in activities with them. It has helped our morale so much. We even make a special effort to look well for these occasions! Videoconferencing means we are no longer isolated. We are now part of a bigger community."

This island school's experience may also stimulate thinking about the potential of videoconferencing for the pastoral care and personal and social development of individual pupils – including the special needs of new immigrants struggling to learn English as a second language.

B. CURRICULUM ENRICHMENT: ACCESS TO EXPERTS

Case Study 7
Politics: Post-16

In May, 1999, 70 A level Politics pupils from four schools in Omagh and Strabane (Omagh Christian Brothers, Omagh Loreto Convent, Strabane Convent Grammar and St. Colman's High School, Strabane) came together in the WELB Technology Education Centre (TEC) for a videoconference link up with the House of Representatives in Washington, DC. Here they had a virtual meeting with a senior US politician, Congressman Jim Walsh. They were also linked simultaneously to grade 12 pupils from a New Jersey high school. The objectives were to deepen the Northern Ireland pupils' understanding of the US constitution which formed part of their A level syllabus, and the New Jersey pupils' knowledge of the situation in Northern Ireland and of the British political system, by giving them "live" audiovisual contact with primary sources of information. The WELB pupils had prepared detailed questions which had been sent in advance to the Congressman's office. The US pupils had also supplied their questions on the NI situation. These were responded to respectively by Congressman Walsh and Dr. Arthur Aughey, senior lecturer in Politics at the University of Ulster, who had joined the WELB pupils in Omagh.

The pupils had the opportunity to interact socially with their trans-Atlantic peers before the start of the meeting. This proved to be fun and visibly eased the understandable nervous tension. Following this, a panel of four pupils from each school asked a range of prepared questions. When these were dealt with by the experts, a roving radio microphone was used to allow the larger group of pupils to participate. This led to some lively and challenging debate on a wide range of issues. Commenting on the success of the virtual meeting, Congressman Walsh said: "This has been a most exciting experience for me. It is the first time I have ever spoken to students in two continents at the same time. I didn't know it was possible yet! We often refer to the Atlantic as the 'Pond'. Today has shown just how small that pond has become!"

Teachers and pupils alike were enthused about having interactive access to an expert in real time and applauded spontaneously when the meeting ended. One teacher described it as "the best thing that has happened in the study of A level politics in the 20 years that I have been teaching the subject". Pupils stated that it had given them a deeper understanding of American politics and had broadened their horizons by letting them see our own situation from a different perspective. Teachers also commented on the improvement in their pupils' presentation, communication and listening skills as a result of preparing for and participating in the videoconference, their enhanced motivation and self-esteem.

The main success factors in this videoconference were: aligning the learning objectives with the A level syllabus, thorough preparation of content and questions, pre-testing of the technology, meticulous organisation and implementation of the complex virtual encounter, including preparing an agreed agenda, and careful chairing of the discussion to encourage adherence to videoconferencing etiquette and to ensure a lively and balanced discussion and a fair hearing for all.

In April 2000, a similar access-to-expert videoconference was organised by the WELB at the request of two schools (Omagh Academy and Mount Lourdes Grammar School, Enniskillen) who were studying the Irish constitution in their A level syllabus. This time the expert was the then Minister for Health and Education in Dáil Éireann, Mr Mícheál Martin. This meeting was equally successful. Teachers and pupils appreciated the opportunity to gain authentic, up-to-the minute information on an important section of their A level studies.

Case Study 8
Literacy and History – Storytelling: KS 3

This is a further example of schools on both sides of the Atlantic linking by videoconference to share an expert. Using the school's own videoconferencing system, Key Stage 3 pupils from St. Joseph's High School, Derry, who were studying Native American history and culture were linked with a mainly African-American school in New Jersey for a storytelling session with the Deputy Chief of the Cherokees who was visiting the American school. The learning objectives were to enhance understanding of Native American history and culture and to improve their communication and presentation skills. The focus was on the storytelling tradition in the three cultures, with particular emphasis on the Native American tradition.

The structure of the lesson is included here to give an idea of the variety of activities and the high degree of interactivity designed into the lesson:

- ▶ courtesy greetings and brief exchange of information about the schools by the two principals;
- ▶ a short talk about the Cherokee nation by the Deputy Chief;
- ▶ a question and answer session;
- ▶ a Cherokee tale told by the Deputy Chief;
- ▶ interaction between the storyteller and the pupils at both sites;
- ▶ an Irish Halloween ghost story told by the school librarian, a noted local storyteller;
- ▶ interaction between the storyteller and the US students;
- ▶ pupils from each school telling stories they had researched among their local communities;
- ▶ a final question and answer session with the Deputy Chief;
- ▶ arrangements for follow-up questions and discussions by email.

Teachers and pupils on both sides of the Atlantic attested to the enhanced understanding of the subject area and the improvement in communication and presentation skills achieved by the videoconference. Added to these benefits were increased motivation (one Derry pupil stated that his appetite had been "whetted" to learn more about the Cherokees), the enjoyment of the learning process, enhanced self-esteem and greater awareness and appreciation of cultural diversity.

Again, detailed preparation and a high degree of interactivity during the link-up were key success factors. The preparation involved a series of emails between the teachers in the two schools on the themes for creative writing, between the pupils from both schools for social introductions, and between the Deputy Chief and the pupils on the Cherokee websites to be researched to ensure a basic awareness of the culture. This helped establish a good relationship in advance of the virtual face-to-face meeting. The pupils also prepared by researching the Irish storytelling tradition and by practice videoconferences to help them improve their self-presentation and communication skills.

Case Study 9
Literacy – Storytelling: KS 3

A trans-Atlantic storytelling videoconference, which exploited the visual capability of the technology and greatly enhanced the important "soft" presentation and communication skills and the self-esteem of the participants, was held between WELB schools in Tyrone and Fermanagh, schools in New Jersey, and an African-American storyteller from the Smithsonian Museum in Washington, DC. The objectives were to improve creative writing and oral presentation skills, to promote personal development and to enhance appreciation of cultural diversity. The focus was the storytelling tradition in both African-American and Irish cultures and the theme was the weaving of identities into fabrics for garments.

The lesson format is included to illustrate how the lesson was designed to ensure variety of pace and activity – slower for storytelling, quicker for the comments and questions of the interactive sessions. The lesson was also designed to take advantage of the visual and interactive characteristics of videoconferencing. Camera close-ups were used to show the colours and the patterns of the clothing in detail, and also to allow the young listeners to enjoy the wonderful non-verbal facial cues which were part of the African-American storyteller's repertoire of communication skills. The main elements of the lesson were:

- ▶ an overview of the 'Wrapped in Kente Exhibit' which was then on display in the Smithsonian and was presented by officials of the museum;
- ▶ a question and answer session involving both sets of pupils;
- ▶ introduction of the African-American story teller, wearing a magnificent ceremonial robe of the traditional Kente material on loan from the museum;

- ▶ telling the story of the origin of Kente and how it met the people's need to express their identity;
- ▶ interactive session between the storyteller and both sets of pupils;
- ▶ Irish pupils, wearing Aran sweaters and Donegal tweeds, telling stories composed by themselves to illustrate the significance of these garments;
- ▶ interactive session with all participants;
- ▶ US African-American students, wearing clothing typical of different African peoples, telling stories they had composed about these peoples;
- ▶ question and answer session involving all participants;
- ▶ brief interactive storytelling workshop, involving constructive comments by the professional storyteller on pupil performance and communication skills and hints for further improvement.

The learning outcomes were regarded as highly satisfactory by the teachers in both schools. Improvements in writing skills and presentation skills and enhanced appreciation of cultural diversity were accompanied by enjoyment of the learning process and by the motivation of presenting to a "live" audience. Improved listening skills and increased self-esteem were outcomes of the actual videoconference. These were important outcomes, as a few of the young pupils were initially camera shy and one had temporarily withdrawn from participation during an early practice session. She gradually gained confidence during the later practice sessions – four were held in all – and in her written feedback after the actual videoconference she stated: "It was the proudest day of my life. To think that I actually told a story by videoconference to a whole class in an American school! I was so nervous before it but felt really good about having done it."

The success factors were both pedagogical and technical. Very focused preparation took place on both written and oral communication – including the practice videoconferences between the pupils and WELB literacy support staff who coached the pupils in the important "soft" social and communication skills. In addition, several pre-tests of the equipment were held.

Case Study 10
Global citizenship/Peer counselling: Post-16

This case study offers what is, perhaps, a unique example of authentic responsible global citizenship and peer counselling that could only have been achieved by videoconferencing. In the aftermath of what has become known as "9/11", the WELB was approached by two New York schools situated only two blocks away from Ground Zero which had been extensively damaged in the atrocity and were in the painful process of re-opening. The idea was to use videoconferencing to connect the young Americans with young people from Omagh, who had experienced the horrendous bomb of 1998, in order to enable peer healing to take place. The videoconference was held on Global Youth Services Day, April 26, 2002. The students from the Ground Zero schools had witnessed the atrocity as it was happening. They wanted to tell their story. They wanted their "young voices" to be heard. The videoconference gave them that opportunity. It also allowed them to listen to other young voices telling of very similar experiences and sharing their coping strategies.

The conference opened with a letter of support from Senator Hillary Clinton. She expressed her hope that, by coming together through videoconferencing to share their painful experiences, the young people of New York and of Omagh would be healed and their spirits strengthened. Videoconferencing proved to be the ideal technology for this purpose. The young people at both sites had a strong sense of presence and felt it was a genuine encounter with "real people" whom they could see and hear and with whom they could empathise. They told and listened to one another's stories. At the end of the conference, the young Americans said they were greatly helped by the courage and resilience of the young participants at the Omagh site, and uplifted by the message of hope they had received from peers, some of whom had been seriously injured, and all of whom had been traumatised to some degree by the Omagh bomb.

Case Study 11
Global citizenship/Peer counselling: Post-16

Another example of peer counselling and peer support was the Virtual Global Youth Forum which was held at regular intervals in 2002. Videoconferencing was used to enable communities of young people from different parts of the world to come together virtually to discuss issues of major interest to them The young people involved were from Northern Ireland (Omagh Youth Club), South Africa and the US Their wide-ranging agenda included drug abuse, AIDS, cultural diversity, teenage pregnancy, under-age drinking, the perceived increase in anti-social behaviour, and the pressures on young people in the modern world. They developed a strong sense of community as they compared how issues were dealt with in the three very different parts of the world and counselled and supported one another according to their various skills and experiences.

The main success factors here were the positive attitude of the youth leaders to videoconferencing, their quickly acquired ability to chair the complex discussions between the three sites, the technical support and training in the skills and behaviours required for videoconferencing provided by the WELB, the authentic nature of the encounters in that the young participants were able to see and hear one another in real time, and the fact that the issues discussed were "real world" and immediately relevant to them.

Case Study 12
Citizenship development project: Post-16

A more formal approach to using videoconferencing for citizenship was the cross-border, cross-community, curriculum project devised by the WELB and St. Angela's College, Sligo, and funded by the European Union Special Support Programme for Peace and Reconciliation. Phase I involved 18 post-primary schools, nine on each side of the border; 28 schools participated in Phase II. The age group was 16+. The aim of the project was to prepare pupils for responsible citizenship by developing the knowledge, skills and attitudes that contribute to mutual understanding and respect for differences. In addition to classroom-based work, cross-community and cross-border pupil encounter on a residential basis was an important feature of the project. Videoconferencing was used by the programme co-ordinators for planning and administration purposes. It was optional for the schools and was used by eight of the original 18 schools.

Common objectives for the use of this technology were agreed. These included using the virtual meetings to enable pupils to establish a good rapport before the residential meetings took place, to help them come to a better understanding of their own beliefs and perceptions of identity and those of others, and to foster meaningful discussions between pupils on sensitive citizenship issues.

The evaluation of the programme found that videoconferencing was a most effective means of breaking down barriers between schools from different communities in that it provided a safe space for the discussion of sensitive issues, while enabling young people to relate more easily to one another. It also noted that the safe space allowed students to express strongly opposing views without animosity, and gave them the opportunity to listen and hear, without feeling threatened, the story of their "opponents". The evaluation found that this led to a marked difference in the reactions to the pupil residential from pupils who had the videoconferencing experience and those who had not. The former were more confident, more positive and derived greater benefit than the latter. The pupils who had met one another virtually before meeting face-to-face reported that videoconferencing had contributed greatly to their positive attitude to the project in general and to the residential in particular and to the benefits they derived from participation.

The success of videoconferencing in this project came from a number of factors: the collaborative planning and setting of clear objectives for using the technology, recognising and exploiting the potential of videoconferencing to facilitate both social and educational exchanges, carefully scaffolding the students, and sensitive chairing of challenging discussions.

Case Study 13:
Health education/Substance abuse: KS 4

Two examples of the use of videoconferencing to support health education in the specific area of substance abuse – one with a US rehabilitation centre and one with a panel of local NI experts – will illustrate how the technology can enrich and extend learning by enabling authentic beyond-the-classroom interactive experiences in real time.

The first of these had an international dimension. St. Patrick's High School, Omagh, joined up via videoconference with a high school in New Jersey to explore the issue of substance abuse among young people. The American school had secured the support of Integrity House, New Jersey, a drugs rehabilitation centre for young addicts. In advance of the virtual visit, the Director of Integrity House had emailed a questionnaire to the Omagh and New Jersey pupils to ascertain the level of their awareness and/or experience of the issue and had used the responses to help shape the agenda.

After preliminary introductions and some social chat, the grim reality of the effects of substance abuse was tackled. Four young recovering addicts from Integrity House told their stories. They spoke about their families. They described their life on the streets and in prison, explained how they had got hooked and told of their hopes of getting clean and making something of their lives. This made a great impact on the Omagh pupils, who then engaged in earnest discussion chaired by the Director, both with the young former addicts and with the New Jersey high school pupils. All of them were strengthened in their resolve to resist the pressures to experiment with drugs in any form.

The outstanding success of this videoconference was due very largely to the careful preparation undertaken by the Director of the rehabilitation centre and his tailoring of the event to the needs of the pupils. The fact that the "lesson" was structured to allow the young people to interact and engage seriously with one another was another important factor. There was no "talking head", no passive absorption of information. The potential of videoconferencing to allow a meaningful interactive face-to-face encounter in real time was fully exploited.

Case Study 14
Health education/Substance abuse: KS 4

The next example is of a cross-border (Ireland) videoconference held in 1998 to mark European Drugs Prevention Week. The WELB initiated a drugs debate with young people north and south of the border. It was an ambitious multi-point conference. The aim was to raise awareness of the existence and very real dangers of drug abuse, and to focus on ways of preventing this happening where possible. Six schools were linked to one another and to a panel of experts at Magee University College. The panel included representatives from the Addiction Unit in the Northlands Centre in Derry, Magilligan Prison, the Western Drugs Action Team and WELB officers. The pupils put their views to the panel and questioned the members on a range of drug related issues.

Success factors in this videoconference included setting up real-world contacts with whom the pupils would want to engage, very careful pre-testing of the technology, the school-based preparation of the questions which were sent in advance to the panel, the good rapport established with the pupils by the panel, who were all used to dealing with young people, and the opportunity for free discussion following the formal question and answer session.

Case Study 15
History, culture and technology literacy: KS 2

A good example of the potential of videoconferencing to enrich the learning experience of primary school pupils through access to experts took place recently (2007) in Parkhall PS, Co. Antrim, in relation to History, Culture, and Technology Literacy. The school was motivated by the need to raise its level of technology literacy. With the active support and encouragement of C2k and of the NEELB Assistant Technology Advisory Officer, Peter Simpson, the classroom teacher – enthusiastically supported by her job-sharing partner – willingly agreed to undertake a major videoconferencing project. She saw how videoconferencing, together with other technologies, had the potential to enrich their P6 history curriculum, the focus of which at the time was Ancient Egypt. She also realised how it could support changes in her teaching to meet the requirements of the revised curriculum, and how it could raise pupils' knowledge and understanding of ICT. She set these as her learning objectives. Pupils used the Internet to research a topic in groups and as a whole class, and to develop thinking and problem solving skills. Videoconferencing provided the pupils with an authentic beyond-the-classroom learning experience through virtually meeting, and interviewing "live", an Egyptologist based in Liverpool World Museum. To further enrich the learning experience, the school decided to include their Education for Mutual Understanding (EMU) partner school, St. Joseph's PS, Antrim, in the link and, with appropriate technical support from NEELB and C2k, a multipoint link was established between the two schools and the expert. Parents and guests joined the other classes in the assembly hall of the school where the event was projected onto a large screen. It was also streamed live from the school's own website to make it available asynchronously to a wider audience.

The teacher found that the project offered many benefits to her pupils. The latter were keenly motivated to learn more about Ancient Egypt, subsequently visiting local libraries or using home computers to research in their own time. With appropriate scaffolding, pupils were able to manage many elements of the project themselves, including some of the technical aspects. This gave them a sense of ownership of the learning process, which contributed greatly to their self-esteem and career aspirations – some have said they would now like to pursue a career in media! They also developed their communicating and teamwork skills in the preparation for the event. From the experience, the teacher learned that "it's ok to let children take the lead. I now know I don't have to be the sage on the stage all the time." She is also now highly motivated to extend her knowledge about the capabilities of videoconferencing.

She identifies the success factors as at-the-elbow technical support for a complex operation, thorough technical preparation, rethinking teaching strategies, and whole school and community support.

Case Study 16
Mathematics/Science/Technology: KS 2

Another stimulating and highly motivating use of videoconferencing at primary school level is the example of the now annual video link-up between Portstewart PS and the National Aeronautics and Space Administration (NASA) in the US. This school came to videoconferencing from a base of highly developed technology literacy. It already had a radio station and a television station that were integrated into the daily life of the school, so videoconferencing seemed to be the logical progression. Once again, support from the Assistant Technology Adviser, Peter Simpson, played a major role. Contact was made with NASA through their website, and the videoconferences were integrated with the P6 maths, science and technology project called "Aliens". The preparation for these virtual encounters is quite challenging, involving research into NASA and working with NASA on composing and articulating questions to be sent in advance of the videoconference. This exercise helps promote higher level thinking and the ability to ask meaningful questions of general relevance. The implementation of the project each year constantly challenges the pupils' creative thinking and problem-solving skills. This experience of "hard fun" virtual learning is greatly enjoyed by the pupils. The school has built up a good relationship with NASA and is now in its third year of collaboration with the Administration. It now benefits from an amendment to NASA's education outreach policy. When Portstewart PS first linked up with NASA, it had to pay a fee of $200 (approximately £100). Now NASA offers its programmes free of charge. This makes it an attractive option for schools. An interesting feature of the Portstewart project to date is that it is basically facilitated by simple videophone technology which the school obtained from participation in the Dissolving Boundaries project. The hope is, of course, to upgrade this, but much has already been achieved by thorough preparation, creative teaching and interactive learning strategies, the opportunity to build up a relationship with NASA at the preparation stage, and good technology support for the actual link-up.

C. COLLABORATIVE DISTANCE LEARNING

Inter-school collaboration: Primary schools

In the context of the European Union (EU) Comenius Education Programme, much good practice in the use of videoconferencing developed at primary level. This programme encourages multi-lateral school partnerships of at least three schools in different European jurisdictions working collaboratively on a curriculum based project. One case study is offered as an example of how videoconferencing facilitated collaborative working across three European countries.

Case Study 17
History/Geography/Literacy: KS 2

In 1999, Irvinestown PS in Co. Fermanagh made very imaginative use of multi-point videoconferencing with their partner schools in Denmark and Italy. At appropriate stages in their project, the schools 'met' virtually to share their work and the teachers used the videoconference to plan the next phase. Their project, which was on the theme of 'Who we are/ Where we live', was developed as an integral part of the KS2 syllabus. The objectives were to give the pupils a sense of place, to widen their horizons, and to raise awareness and appreciation of cultural diversity.

Teachers were enthused about the learning outcomes of these virtual encounters. Pupils were highly motivated by the prospect of presenting their work to a "live" audience. There was also the enrichment of the input of the Danish and Italian schools in the areas of History and Geography. The working language of the videoconferences was English, which the pupils in the other two schools were learning as part of their primary curriculum. This placed a responsibility on the Irvinestown pupils as the only native speakers of the language. They had to ensure that their English was clear, grammatically accurate and clearly articulated and that they wrote and spoke in simple, well-constructed sentences. As a result, they gained in literacy, communication and presentation skills. They also gained an awareness of different languages and cultures and a very positive attitude to them, as each session included a "how do you say?" question and answer encounter, and tapes of basic greetings in the various languages were exchanged by the schools.

The principal pointed out how valuable this experience was to his pupils, most of whom had never been out of Northern Ireland and were not likely to be in the near future. In addition to aligning the learning objectives to the curriculum, the good preparation and the interactive nature of the virtual encounter, three important success factors in this collaboration were: the enthusiasm of the teachers in all the schools who felt they had gained greatly in professional development through collaborating with their European colleagues; the whole school support given to the videoconferencing element of the project, and the support of parents and members of the local community, many of whom attended the videoconferences as observers.

Case Study 18
Literacy/Sharing favourite stories: KS 2

A more recent example taken from the primary sector demonstrates how regular collaboration through videoconferencing across the Atlantic enriched the curriculum, widened horizons, and helped primary children enjoy the learning process. In February, 2004, from the WELB Technology Education Centre, St. Conor's PS, Omagh, linked into the classroom of an elementary school in Pittsburgh for a six-week literacy project delivered by videoconferencing. The aim was to encourage reading for pleasure. The theme was sharing favourite stories and legends. The schools took turns in introducing their partner to their selected story. The children explained why they had chosen it. The teacher read the story, using the document camera to show the colourful illustrations to the pupils at the distant site. Following this, the session became very interactive, with questions and answers and opinions about the plot, the characters and the pictures coming from the children at both sites, often accompanied by much laughter. An interesting feature of these weekly virtual encounters was that the children on both sides soon forgot about the technology and began to act as if they were in the same classroom.

This promoted a good relationship between them and an experience of learning as fun. They seized the visual opportunities afforded by the technology to enliven the presentation and entertain one another, by dressing up occasionally as the characters in their story, and adding songs and dance to their presentations.

The teacher factor was key to the success of this videoconferencing project. The teachers were enthusiastic about the collaboration, worked together to plan each virtual encounter, and quickly learned to use the technology very creatively. They rose to the challenge of engaging the children at both their own site and in the distant classroom. They used body language very effectively for the storytelling and structured the lesson in such a way as to ensure variety and interactivity. They were delighted with the outcomes of the virtual experience. These included a new enthusiasm for reading on the part of the pupils, their increased awareness and enjoyment of other cultures, and greatly enhanced self-esteem as a result of their very positive virtual experiences.

Inter-school collaboration: Post-primary schools

The following case studies are offered as examples of good practice in promoting collaborative learning in the post-primary sector.

Case Study 19
History in the "virtual shared classroom": KS 3

In this project, using mainly videoconferencing, two schools in Northern Ireland (Thornhill College and St. Joseph's College, Derry) each shared a virtual classroom with a partner school in New Jersey. The learning objective was to enhance understanding of aspects of the history curriculum. Each pair of schools jointly planned lessons on topics common to their curricula. One pair of schools collaborated on a project on the American West; the other two worked together on aspects of the Holocaust. The partners met once a week by videoconference for a period of six weeks. The lessons were pupil-centred and highly interactive. The pupils collaborated by email in preparation for the lessons and exchanged information, including relevant websites. During each shared lesson, the two classes acted as one, dividing into mixed groups of Irish and American pupils. They made joint presentations of their work, and interacted both with the content and with their "classmates". The schools also shared visiting experts. In addition to deepening their knowledge and understanding of the topic under study, the pupils improved noticeably in self-confidence, in communication and presentation skills and in the ability to work with others in a virtual environment.

Teacher enthusiasm was again a major success factor in this project which required a significant commitment of time and energy to detailed joint preparation. Another significant factor was the shift in their pedagogy as a result of using videoconferencing. They recognised and exploited its potential to enable pupils to take more collaborative responsibility for their own learning – and to enjoy the process.

Case Study 20
Japanese studies project: Post-16

This project which started in 1990 as the Japanese Language programme is an example of how advances in technology, when used with appropriate pedagogy, can impact beneficially on the learning experience. From an early stage, David Farrell, Vice-principal of Ballyclare Secondary School, was the driving force, first as Education Officer to the project and later as consultant, in promoting the project and sustaining its momentum. The aim initially was to broaden the 6th form curriculum through the inclusion of the Japanese language. At this stage, email was emerging as a viable technology for electronic links. It was used to link the Northern Ireland schools in the project with 10 schools in Japan in order to provide an authentic cultural link. This led in 1993 to the broadening of the programme – under a new name – The Japanese Studies project – to include language, the strengthening of email links and the study of Japanese culture. In 1996-1997, the project moved from being heavily dependent on email to exploring the potential of videoconferencing technology. The teachers found that this offered a stimulating audiovisual means of communication in real time. The early videoconferences proved to be extremely motivating to pupils. In 1999, a more structured approach was designed. This required the pupils to engage in a collaborative, student-led, skills-based assignment involving the detailed costing and planning of a trip to each other's country.

More recently, to overcome the major obstacle to meaningful communication, that of language, a concrete problem-solving assignment was designed. The challenge was to solve the problem of how a small robotic car could travel a maximum distance at an optimum speed using a limited amount of fuel. Pupils collaborated via videoconferencing and the Internet and exchanged information, using critical thinking and problem-solving skills at a high level, expressed mainly in the "international language" of robotics, advanced mathematics and technology.

Videoconferencing has become fully integrated into the Japanese Studies class. David Farrell and his colleagues have identified three phases leading to this integration:

▶ asynchronous email for initial self-introductions to real-time interactive peer education on Japanese language using video-conferencing and second language communication;

▶ showing and discussing authentic artefacts and material to exploit the audiovisual characteristics of videoconferencing, to increase the pupils' level of comfort with the technology and promote cultural awareness;

▶ the "Let's do it" phase: interaction on a more sophisticated scale that is student-led and student centred. At this stage, pupils are given responsibility for organizing and planning the video-conference and designing interactive work. They gain a sense of the social presence of their distant peers and an experience of working as a single group, though separated by thousands of miles.

David Farrell's experience with videoconferencing in the Japanese Studies project has led him to view this technology as a valuable learning tool which needs to be introduced systematically and progressively. He sees the teacher's responsibility as ensuring high quality planning and organising in the preparation period and, equally importantly, educating pupils in the use of videoconferencing and then allowing them to use it in a constructive learning environment.

Inter-school collaboration: Special schools

Case Study 21
My Town project: KS 3

The Learning Northern Ireland-based "My Town" project (2005-2006) involved two schools for pupils with severe learning difficulties (SLD) in different parts of Northern Ireland – Clifton School in Bangor and Kilronan School in Magherafelt. The pupils involved were in KS3 and had a wide range of severe learning difficulties. In terms of collaborative work, the psychological distance between such pupils and distant peers tended to be perceived as almost unbridgeable. Traditionally, such schools have tended to emphasize adaptive or assistive technologies, such as alternative keyboards (touch screen, large print), alternative mouse devices (switches), and software such as writing with symbols and text-to-speech, in order to enable individual pupils to engage with computer technology. This project set out to explore the potential of desktop text- and video-conferencing to enable and enhance distance collaborative learning in the SLD environment. The project was aligned with elements of the geography curriculum. The focus was "My Town". The aim was to give pupils a sense of their own and other places, using ICT as a bridge to the world outside the classroom. The more able children used symbol-assisted software to engage in text-conferencing with their partner school. They also communicated once a week by videoconferencing.

The outcomes of using videoconferencing technology were very encouraging. It was inclusive of all the children, including those with little or no oral skills who used body language to communicate, or had their more articulate peers interpret for them. It increased their motivation and improved their concentration. They worked enthusiastically at classroom activities connected with the project, and some endeavored to improve keyboard skills to keep communication going through the week. Children with behavioral difficulties remained totally attentive and engaged throughout the 30-minute sessions. Both classes perceived videoconferencing as fun. They were proactive in the physical preparations in the classroom, voluntarily helping the teacher arrange chairs round the monitor, and ensuring that the microphone was to hand. A surprise finding was that videoconferencing fostered a sense of community and an enthusiasm for collaborative work, not only between the partner schools, but also within each classroom. This was evidenced in the artefacts constructed to represent features of the partner school's town which were displayed during the videoconference session, and in the willingness to help one another during the interactive videoconferences. Perhaps the most significant finding was that the children gained some understanding of the complex concepts of virtual and physical presence. They wanted to meet their on-screen friends in real-life. During the course of the project, the two schools met twice physically, each school hosting the visit of the other. Both occasions were outstandingly successful in terms of socialisation and sheer enjoyment.

Key success factors were identified as follows:
- ▶ principal and whole school support. This helped overcome many of the logistic problems such as timetabling, and provided the teachers with reassuring support;
- ▶ the provision of training and ongoing support by C2k;
- ▶ the collaboration of the two classroom teachers on the issue of pedagogy, both being instinctively aware of the need to adapt their methodology and their traditional role to exploit the new learning environment. Their discussions, which frequently included the C2k support officers allocated to the project, generally took place by videoconferencing. The technology proved to be an effective planning tool, as well as enabling the teachers to get to know each other and thus collaborate more effectively;
- ▶ the support of the classroom assistants. A finding of the evaluation was the need to include classroom assistants in any future training for using technology in special needs schools.

Collaborative school networks

Currently, videoconferencing technology is beginning to be recognised in Northern Ireland as a powerful resource for curriculum extension and enrichment among networks of schools. Within the context of the revised curriculum and the curriculum entitlement framework, a collegial approach, funded by the Department of Education, is being piloted in a number of post-primary schools in different areas across Northern Ireland and has resulted in the creation of collaborative learning environments. Two examples – an Irish-medium collaborative project and the Magherafelt Learning Partnership – are given below.

Case Study 22
Irish-medium project – Citizenship: KS 3-4

Funding was received from the Department of Education to install videoconferencing systems for a pilot project exploring the potential of videoconferencing, together with Learning NI, to support collaboration between the three schools involved in Irish Medium education – Coláiste Feirste in Belfast, the Irish-medium unit in St. Catherine's College, Armagh, and the Irish-medium unit in St. Brigid's College, Derry. The pilot project, entitled "Mo Cheantar" (My Area/District), was completed in 2006 during the C2k early videoconferencing pilot phase. At this stage, desktop videoconferencing software, the Polycom PVX, was used for self-presentation and information exchange in real time by the pupils, and for planning purposes, discussions and application sharing by the teachers. In both cases, the real-time, audiovisual aspect of the technology was effective in helping to create a learning community out of the three geographically separated Irish-medium schools in Northern Ireland. Learning NI was used for asynchronous discussions and sharing photos and other graphics.

The teachers reported satisfaction with the experience. Their enthusiasm and commitment to this relatively new concept of collaborative learning across schools and their willingness to explore the potential of the new technologies to deliver it were keys to the success of the project. Among the benefits they identified for pupils were enhancement of technology literacy, enjoyment of technology-mediated collaborative learning, improved social skills through interacting with their peers, independent learning and an enhanced sense of cultural identity. The benefits to the teachers were significant professional development arising from the experience of integrating multi-media in the classroom and from the opportunity for inter-school collaboration in planning and implementing lessons. They also gained a sense of community and sectoral identity. The teachers were encouraged by the potential of the combination of videoconferencing and Learning NI to help them meet the challenges of the revised curriculum and of the curriculum entitlement framework. Following the successful completion of the pilot, and with the recent acquisition of a dedicated videoconferencing unit, the Tandberg 75MXP, the schools are currently working together on a Citizenship pilot for year 8. They are also exploring the possibility of distant teaching across the three schools to extend the curriculum by sharing courses.

In addition to working within the Irish-medium network, Coláiste Feirste, has used videoconferencing, in the context of cross-phase liaison, to team-teach Irish language lessons with a feeder primary school and to extend its horizons by participating in the 2006 Global Run project. This is a global network of schools initiated by a practising teacher in White Plains, New York State, for the purpose of raising cultural awareness and promoting practical action on global issues. Coláiste Feirste's plans for the current school year include the development of links with a college in Galway and a videoconferencing-based project with a school in Japan.

Case Study 23
Magherafelt Learning Partnership

A similar network, the Magherafelt Learning Partnership, embraces all five post-primary schools in the town – St. Mary's, Rainey Endowed, Sperrin Integrated, Magherafelt High School and St. Pius X High School. In the initial pilot phase, the schools used a videoconferencing solution supplied by the NEELB, and with the support and expert guidance of C2k and of the Board's Assistant Technology Advisor, Peter Simpson, they have already collaborated successfully on a number of projects, the objectives of which were to explore the potential of the technology to enhance and extend the curriculum, and generally to expand the horizons of the pupils. One example of this, among many, is the use of videoconferencing in a partnership-wide Careers Conference hosted by St. Mary's. The schools linked up by videoconference with Harvard University. Five pupils from each school, observed by the rest of their peers, questioned the Admissions Officer on entrance requirements and career prospects. Very thorough preparation of pupils and testing of the technology took place prior to the actual event. Questions were prepared in advance by the pupils in class, emailed to Harvard, where they were refined for more general relevance, and returned to the pupils. Pupils were given practice videoconferences to ensure they were comfortable with the technology and aware of the need for interactive engagement.

The principal of one of the schools, reflecting the general opinion, was in no doubt that the very thorough preparation and training of the pupils, together with the technology support and guidance from Peter Simpson, were the success factors in what proved to be a very rich learning experience that widened the horizons of the pupils and raised their expectations and career aspirations. Acknowledging the need to expend significant time on this preparation and training, the principal felt that this was a feature of the early adopter period and would gradually decrease. The teachers remained motivated. They could see the big picture and felt the outcomes were worth the effort. In the case of the Harvard videoconference, the experience not only provided the pupils with up-to-date information from a primary source, but also greatly increased their communication skills, extended their horizons and enhanced their self-confidence.

A second ambitious careers-focused video link was established with an international company in Australia, in which a former pupil of one of the schools was employed. The same format of five pupils from each school, with the full classes observing, was used, and the same careful preparation and training preceded this videoconference. There was an extremely positive reaction to this videoconference from both the panel of pupils and the observers. They were conscious of the value of the authentic information they were receiving. Again, the distant learning experience raised their career aspirations and their awareness that in this digital age, the physical location of the school no longer determined the range or the quality of the learning experiences that could be offered.

Currently, each of the Partnership schools has purchased a dedicated video-conferencing unit. They plan to use this technology to explore its potential to extend the curriculum through delivering high quality distant teaching and learning courses. Their first experiment in this area is to access a course in Law from an external provider in England. This will be taught by multi-point videoconferences to two sets of paired schools, and by point-to-point videoconferencing to one school. They also plan to begin distance teaching by videoconferencing across schools, including a short Graded Objectives in Modern Languages (GOML) course. The schools feel it will be .interesting to compare their endeavours in this area with the lessons bought "off the shelf". Based on the experience of videoconferencing to date, they recognise its potential in terms of enhancing and expanding the curriculum, particularly in the case of minority subjects, in reducing or eliminating pupil and teacher movement by bringing the outside world directly into the classroom audio-visually and in real time, and generally in making possible the ideal of moving information, not people.

Case Study 24
Learning-by-doing: Various Key Stages

Typical of the creative use of videoconferencing, even at this early stage within the Magherafelt Partnership, is the range of projects recently conducted on a learning-by-doing basis by one of the schools – Sperrin Integrated College. The school took advantage of an invitation to join the 2006 Global Run project. With the support of C2k and of Peter Simpson of the NEELB, their Year 13 pupils held a one-hour videoconference with a school in New York, exploiting the visual characteristic of the technology by presenting their school drama. This gave them hands-on experience of using the technology and proved to be highly motivating. The school hopes to take part in Global Run again this year with a group of Year 9 pupils.

Another effective videoconference was based on sharing a storyteller. Drawing on the school's participation in the Dissolving Boundaries project, they linked with their partner school in the Republic of Ireland to share the visit to their school of a renowned storyteller who had formerly been a teacher. The two sets of pupils greatly enjoyed the experience and remained fully engaged throughout the videoconference. The classroom teacher was in no doubt that this was due very largely to the storyteller's understanding of the interactive requirement of good teaching – born of her years in the classroom. Not only did she interact with both the local and the distant class, but also had the two classes interacting with each other. The class teacher also felt that in the process of learning-by-doing, they had discovered an effective three-step method of phasing videoconferencing into the curriculum:

▶ To get started, take advantage of any "one-off" video-conferencing opportunity e.g. Global Run (see Appendix A), sharing experts, a field trip. This engenders excitement and enthusiasm, helps to build relationships and to stimulate creative thinking, especially with regard to collaborative project work between schools, both locally and in other parts of the world.

▶ Later, a more formal approach can be adopted, such as accessing lessons from professional content providers – the school is considering offering German as a minority subject and monitoring this for feasibility. This stage would also include cross-phase teaching, as for example, accessing technology lessons from the local FE College to meet the new curriculum entitlement requirements.

▶ The third stage would involve the sharing of courses by distant teaching across the network of schools.

Virtual field trips

Because of its ability to connect people anywhere in the world audio-visually and in real time, videoconferencing is a highly effective educational tool for extending learning experiences beyond the classroom, without encountering the barriers of distance, cost, time and wear and tear on human energy. Two examples will be given of good practice in this area: an early experiment at post-primary level involving a number of schools coming together in the WELB Technology Education Centre, and a recent one involving an island school sharing its field trip from open space with its US partner.

Case Study 25
Geography virtual field trip: KS 3

In March 1999, as part of a learning-by-doing approach, and following consultation with teachers, the WELB organised a virtual trip from its Technology Education Centre to a packaging plant in Greenville, South Carolina, for pupils from all the post-primary schools in Omagh. The objective was to use videoconferencing to meet one of the requirements of the KS3 Geography syllabus – the study of an economic activity – and to do so in a way that provided an authentic beyond-the-classroom learning experience. The focus of the visit was on the impact of computer technology on the workplace. The Omagh pupils were also linked with peers in a school in New Jersey who "accompanied" them on the trip. During the virtual visit, the pupils were given an interactive tour of the plant and saw on camera a close-up demonstration of the packaging plant's automated operations.

In preparation for this virtual field trip, pupils had retrieved information about the South Carolina plant from the Internet and familiarised themselves with the 'itinerary' and the geography of South Carolina. Follow-up questions were by email between the pupils and the plant tour guide. These covered not only issues specific to the industrial plant, but also areas of social and personal interest.

The thorough school-based preparation, the opportunity for follow-up questions by email, the ability of the technology to exploit the visual aspect of the visit and the excellent communication skills of the tour guide were significant factors in the educational success of this early trip. The immediacy of videoconferencing, the feeling of "almost being there" and the opportunities for interacting with the tour guide motivated the pupils. They identified, however, the need for more social interaction both with their American peers and with the tour guide. This was an important learning point for us with regard to the need to take on board the interactive social aspect when planning and designing a virtual learning experience.

Case Study 26
A shared virtual field trip from open space: KS 2

A more recent (2005) example of virtual field trips, for which I am greatly indebted to Peter Simpson of the NEELB, illustrates the potential offered by advances in technology to share the experience from an actual open space location where there cannot be any ISDN lines or IP connections. The NEELB Creativity Truck facility, a fully equipped outside broadcast vehicle, based on the model of the vehicle used by Ulster Television and initially funded by the European Union's Interreg Program, enables local schools to link with schools in the US and to invite them to join their field trips. The truck brings the equipment needed to televise the field experience. Microwave radio and video links mean that connections can be made from the actual spot to the Truck, from where it can be transferred to the partner school in the US. An example of this is the Rathlin Island project. This project linked the island primary school with an elementary school in Fairfax, Virginia. The environmental expert in Rathlin, who was working with the pupils from the island school, was able to show live video of what he was finding on the seashore and to describe his findings. Pupils in Mantua, Virginia, were able to see this live through the videoconference link, to ask him questions and to interact with their Rathlin Island peers. This enabling of shared virtual field trips from open space has significant implications for the future use of videoconferencing in education.

D. PROFESSIONAL DEVELOPMENT

Professional development for teachers can be facilitated by videoconferencing in a number of ways. The use of the technology for planning and discussing appropriate teaching strategies between teachers involved in collaborative projects creates a "virtual staffroom". Here, they can experience informal, but extremely valuable, professional development, gain in confidence in using the technology and cease to feel isolated from their peers, as is sometimes the case for those teaching minority subjects or working in small rural schools. Instances of this type of professional development have already been noted in Section C.

Videoconferencing has also proved itself a highly effective tool for formal professional development, both within Northern Ireland and on an international basis. Unfortunately, there are only a few limited examples of good practice in this area. As yet, these have not been followed up systematically or embedded in the system. Some of these are included, however, because they show what can be done, because it has already been done successfully, albeit on a small scale and for a short period of time.

Case Study 27
Early and continuing professional development

Early professional development

Beginning in 1998, videoconferencing was used very successfully in the Early Professional Development programme for beginning teachers in Northern Ireland. In one of the first induction programmes held in the Technology Education Centre, Omagh, Dr. Anne Moran of the University of Ulster, who was present at the Jordanstown site, addressed the teachers in Omagh and conducted interactive workshops. This use of videoconferencing was welcomed by teachers, as it enabled them to have the benefit of outside expertise without any additional demands of time or travel.

Inter-Board in-service programme for heads of modern languages

For a number of years the five Education & Library Boards in Northern Ireland developed an innovative training programme for Heads of Modern Languages departments. The programme was divided into a number of modules. These were delivered jointly through videoconferencing to a number of centres throughout Northern Ireland by the Boards' Languages Advisers in partnership with St. Mary's University College, Belfast, which also accredited the training. Each session was carefully structured to ensure variety and pace and included 30 minutes of formal input, 10 minutes for questions and answers, a 15-minute break, another formal input of about 30 minutes, concluding with further questions and answers. PowerPoint presentations were included in the formal input. Teachers and tutors welcomed the saving in time and travel and enjoyed the interactive nature of the training. This model was also successfully used for an A level Religious Education (RE) Inter-Board videoconference. This was arranged by the Boards' RE Advisers in association with the Council for Curriculum, Examinations and Assessment (CCEA). WELB organised the videoconference link-up; the University of Ulster at Magee College hosted an additional site for WELB teachers, and the University of Ulster at Coleraine provided the 'bridge' to connect the six sites where the teachers were present.

International in-service programme for primary mathematics teachers

Through the medium of videoconferencing, a significant international dimension was added to a two-day in-service programme for primary school numeracy co-ordinators when part of it was delivered by a panel of three Mathematics specialists from Carlow University, Pittsburgh. The United States panel, which comprised University faculty and practising teachers, spoke of successful parental involvement projects and of strategies, resources and materials that had proved effective. The panel were also keen to hear of the work being done in numeracy in Northern Ireland, and the local teachers were given the opportunity to share heir own good practice. The exchange of ideas across the Atlantic was described as "exhilarating".

The experience was later made available to post-primary teachers at an in-service course. Plans were made for follow-up by email as the WELB teachers were eager to follow up leads given by their US colleagues. The latter also were keen to pursue some of the successful strategies practised by the WELB teachers. Both sides felt that collaboration could extend to other parts of the curriculum.

The success factors in all these virtual learning experiences for teachers were careful planning of the event by the organisers, drawing up an agreed agenda, pre-testing the system and designing interactive strategies to foster engagement by all present. A further factor was the skilful chairing of the virtual meetings to ensure pace and variety and the completion of the agenda.

E. THE FUTURE

Case Study 28
Virtual day – Mathematics/Science/English: KS 4

This final case study offers us a glimpse of what changes may take place in the school day in the not-too-distant future. Ashfield Girls' High School, Belfast, in collaboration with Ballyclare High School, held a virtual day at school for year 11 pupils in June, 2007. These pupils stayed at home and were connected virtually to school, using Learning NI and a desktop collaboration suite with videocnferencing capabilities (known as Virtual Classroom). The aim of the day was to develop awareness of e-learning opportunities, to promote independent study and to blur the boundaries between school and home. Dedicated videoconferencing systems were used to enable pupils from Ashfield Girls'to collaborate in pupil-led lessons in science, mathematics and English with their peers in Ballyclare High in the Virtual Day experiment. The initial aim had been to see how well home learning could be facilitated by uploading lessons and learning materials to Learning NI. It was later decided to include a videoconferencing element, and to monitor the impact on learning of the enriched virtual learning environment. In terms of preparation and uploading of materials, operating and managing the technologies, and shifting towards strategies that fostered pupil autonomy, this was a steep learning curve for all involved. The desktop software (Virtual Clasroom) was used to link individual pupils working at home by videoconference with their teacher and to enable them to engage in collaborative work with another "distant" pupil. At the end of the day, some of the the pupils using the desktop system joined the plenary videoconference between the two schools to give feedback on their experience.

Pupils were positive about the virtual experience. They particularly enjoyed the independent and collaborative learning that the technology made possible. A young pupil from Ashfield, who was "not into computers – not even computer games!" found the desktop conference system very user-friendly. She also found it ideal for negotiating meaning with other pupils and with the teacher and she particulary valued this experience of learning as a social activity. She stated it was much easier to ask questions via videoconferencing than in the classroom where she would be more easily embarassed – particularly when it was necessary to ask follow-up questions. The same pupil also found that using this technology to learn meant that there were fewer distractions or disruptions. This enabled her to be more focused and to take responsibility for her own learning. Her reaction to the virtual day was: "It just flew! I loved the whole experience."

Teachers saw great potential for this multimedia-rich approach to teaching and learning. The vice-principal of Ashfield felt that it opened up possibilities to do things schools could not do before and to do some things better. One immediate application he could see was the inclusion of pupils who might be unable to attend school because of health or other reasons. He envisaged teaching classes via videoconferencing to allow such pupils to join in from home using a basic desktop system. This, he felt, would help them re-engage socially with classmates as well as keep pace with them academically.. He believed teachers would derive significant professional development from using technology to deliver lessons in this way. Those who taught minority subjects could connect audiovisually in real time with their colleagues in other schools, thus diminishig the sense of isolation that such teachers often feel. Similarly, technology could now facilitate pupil access to minority subjects not available in the school.

The final verdict, given by an objective expert observer who had monitored the virtual day by videoconference from a site in England and who joined in the plenary session, was that "good learning has taken place!"

CHAPTER FOUR:
Successful Videoconferencing

Getting started

Videoconferencing is a very user-friendly technology. Once the appropriate system is installed, the learning curve for operating it is very gentle. Training in the basic end-user skills can be done in a few hours. These skills include:

- ▶ scheduling a session (or placing the call if outside the C2k network);
- ▶ activating the system;
- ▶ receiving a call;
- ▶ making a call;
- ▶ controlling the camera and arranging pre-sets;
- ▶ using the microphone and muting it as appropriate;
- ▶ ending the call.

This is enough to get started. Teachers do not need to wait until they are experts! The important thing is to learn by doing – e.g., by connecting at an early stage with colleagues in a "friendly" school which has videoconferencing capability, and practicing these end-user skills with more experienced colleagues in a relaxed environment. As the need arises, the teacher will learn how to deal with occasional problems, attach peripheral hardware, e.g., document camera, laptop for presentations and sharing resources, and VCR/DVD recorder. Operational skills for these are easily and quickly acquired.

Teachers will also need training or guidance in the logistics of using videoconferencing in the classroom. These include creating a suitable videoconferencing environment, planning, organising and implementing a videoconference. The following suggestions for addressing the logistical element are not exhaustive, but should give some idea of what is involved in the process.

Creating the learning environment

Ideally, the environment for a dedicated system should be a dedicated room. This is seldom the case in practice, but whatever classroom or space is used for videoconferencing should be supportive of learning. To achieve this, the following factors should be kept in mind:

▶ The room should be readily available to potential participants. A room that is in frequent use for other purposes will obviously raise serious issues of accessibility.

▶ It should be large enough to accommodate comfortably the proposed numbers of participants and to make it possible to seat them so that they can see the monitor – usually a large television screen and/or whiteboard or a data projector image – and be seen by participants at the far site. This is essential to keep the pupils engaged.

▶ It should be located away from noisy corridors, gymnasiums, canteens, or other external sources of noise, so as not to confuse the camera which may be voice-activated – configured to follow sound. Videoconferencing systems are usually equipped with extremely sensitive microphones that pick up all sounds, both internal and external.

▶ Choose artificial lighting over natural lighting as it is easier to control. Make sure the lighting falls on the faces of participants.

▶ Do not seat participants in front of a window as they would be seen in silhouette.

▶ Avoid "busy" backgrounds with many colours, posters, etc. Use a plain coloured screen – preferably blue – to mask this. Use a logo or text to identify the site.

▶ Try to limit the amount of background noise and echo in the room, because sound quality is even more important than picture quality in a videoconference.

▶ Turn off all monitors that may be in the room to eliminate distracting visual content.

▶ Ideally, the camera should be placed just above the monitor showing the far site.

▶ Use the picture-in-picture (the small picture of your own site) to check what exactly you are transmitting, and adjust accordingly. Remember that the participants at the far site will see only what the camera sees.

Taking account of these factors will help participants experience videoconferencing as a transparent technology, i.e. one that functions so smoothly that learners become unaware of it and focus on the learning event.

Checklist for planning and organising a videoconference

When planning a videoconference it is important to work closely with your link partner(s) in preparation for the actual event. It is advisable to make contact some weeks in advance of the actual videoconference. The following suggestions will help start the planning process:

- ▶ Decide together on the learning goal. Identify which elements of the curriculum requirements the videoconference will address.
- ▶ Ensure that a teacher or videoconferencing facilitator will be present at the far site.
- ▶ Discuss and design strategies for interaction with your link partner.
- ▶ Plan the date and time of the videoconference carefully. Allow a sufficient period for preparation. Check time zones where appropriate.
- ▶ Decide on the duration of the videoconference.
- ▶ Decide on the layout of the room.
- ▶ Check the availability of the videoconferencing system – and the room – before finalising the date and time.
- ▶ Schedule the call to connect all participants at the agreed date and time. (If outside the C2k network, for a multi-point conference, i.e. where more than two sites are involved, make arrangements for a 'bridge' or gateway. This is a centre which connects all sites in a videoconference.)
- ▶ Plan the agenda together, preferably using videoconferencing to "meet" with your partner. The use of videoconferencing at this stage offers many benefits.
  - It can serve as a technical test of the equipment – this pre-testing of the technology is an essential part of the preparation.
  - It gives partners an opportunity to familiarise themselves with the videoconferencing system.

- It builds up a good relationship between them, thereby helping ensure a successful videoconference-mediated learning event.

▶ Practise using the software or videoconferencing unit as often as possible before the actual session to build confidence.

▶ Decide on the number taking part and on the structure or format of the conference. The size of the group may be determined by the nature of the videoconference, the physical space available and the type of system being used. It is usually advisable to work with a small group to encourage engagement and interactivity. With large groups, e.g. a whole class, it is better to select a panel of main participants to deal with the core issues and to ask the key questions. It is also helpful to allow time at the end for an open discussion to follow the panel discussion in order to provide others present with an opportunity to become involved.

▶ Ensure that all participants are aware in advance of the specific focus of the conference and have familiarised themselves with the areas to be covered.

▶ Where appropriate, i.e. when dealing with a panel of speakers or with an individual expert, send core questions or issues in advance.

▶ Ensure that all working documents to be used during the videoconference are sent out in advance to all participants. This allows time for the documents to be studied prior to the videoconference and makes for a more productive encounter.

▶ Arrange for practice videoconferences for pupils where appropriate. This allows them to become familiar with the technology as well as enabling them to improve their presentation and communication skills. If possible, record the practice. This can be used to improve the quality of participation and add value to the whole experience.

▶ Any visual aids, e.g. PowerPoint presentation, maps, photos, texts, slides, video clips or artefacts, should be included in the practice. All printed documents should be of similar layout in order to limit camera refocusing.

▶ Involve the far site facilitator in the practice sessions.

▶ Complete the final draft of the agreed agenda and send a copy to your link school. This ensures a common understanding of the programme and procedures to be followed during the videoconference.

▶ Prepare PowerPoint or any visual aids in a format and resolution appropriate to videoconferencing technology.

Application sharing

The following suggestions for sharing applications should help:

▶ Use landscape format (not portrait) and leave a 10% border.

▶ Font size should be 24-40.

▶ Recommended fonts are Times New Roman, Arial (or any sans serif fonts).

▶ Use light coloured text against a dark background. Yellow text on a blue background works very well.

▶ A rule of thumb known as "the rule of seven" is worth considering. Limit slides or documents to seven lines of text and seven words per line. If appropriate to needs, an even more effective configuration is the "four by six" – four lines of text with six words per line, or vice versa.

▶ The golden rule is to keep it simple and uncluttered. The "bells and whistles" approach is not appropriate for presentations by videoconferencing.

▶ When showing recordings, remember that high amounts of movement require extra bandwidth to be transmitted.

▶ Avoid shiny or glossy paper in visuals.

Before the videoconference

The following practical tips relate to the days immediately prior to the videoconference:

▶ Schedule any test call required.

▶ Schedule the session. (NB. If outside the C2k network, exchange ISDN/IP numbers with link partner(s) and be sure to arrange for at least one test call.)

▶ Have the name and telephone number of a contact person at the far site to enable contact in case of difficulties.

▶ Although most videoconferencing systems are becoming increasingly user-friendly, for a major videoconference it is generally advisable to have technical back-up. This frees the teacher/chairperson to attend to the smooth running of the conference.

▶ Where appropriate, arrange for recording and/or video-streaming of the actual videoconference. This can be a valuable education resource, particularly if a specialist or a panel of experts has been involved. It can be archived for future use and can also be viewed by pupils who may have missed the actual videoconference.

On the day of the videoconference

▶ If the videoconference system is not located in your room, plan to arrive at the venue about 15 minutes before starting time.

▶ Have the call details and contact numbers to hand.

▶ Check the lay-out of the room.

▶ Check that the camera is placed just above the monitor. Arrange camera pre-sets.

▶ Activate the picture-in-picture (self-view window) to view what the far site is seeing. Adjust camera as necessary.

▶ Check that the microphones are appropriately placed to pick up audio from speakers. Remember that audio quality is even more important than picture quality in a videoconference.

▶ Check that all required peripheral hardware – e.g. document camera, laptop or PC, Whiteboard – are connected.

▶ Greet arriving participants and ensure that they are appropriately seated. Because of the landscape format of the camera, and to avoid excessive camera movement, keep groups sitting together.

▶ Address participants by name. If appropriate, ask them to display their name cards.

▶ Distribute copies of the agenda and any other relevant documents.

▶ Make sure participants are aware of the basic etiquette of videoconferencing. (See the final section of this chapter.)

▶ Emphasise the need for interaction with their colleagues at the far site.

▶ Power on unit, or launch desktop software, at least 10 minutes before the videoconference is due to start.

▶ Check that the sound and picture quality are satisfactory at both (all) sites.

▶ Arrange for microphones to be muted during the conference when someone is speaking from the link site. This simple procedure provides for significantly better sound quality.

▶ People like to see the face of the person talking. This is one of the strengths of videoconferencing. Try to ensure that the camera is always on the speaker. This helps sustain the interest and engagement of distant participants.

▶ Make sure that participants understand the importance of looking at the camera when interacting with the far site.

During the videoconference: The role of the teacher/chair

A good videoconference does not just happen. One important factor in ensuring success is good directing and facilitating by the teacher/chairperson. The following suggestions may help those who undertake this vital role:

▶ Begin the videoconference punctually.

▶ Encourage social interaction at the start to establish a good rapport between the participants.

▶ Adhere to the agenda to avoid confusion.

▶ Show enthusiasm for the learning event. Participants pick up on this.

▶ Ensure the camera is on the speaker – not necessarily in close-up, unless it is the guest speaker. Focusing the camera on a 2-4 person group is adequate for a speaker "from the floor".

▶ Keep strictly to time. This ensures that the programme is completed and that those who had prepared contributions have the opportunity to share them. Young pupils can be very disappointed if their prepared contribution has to be dropped.

▶ Use verbal transitions between sections, i.e., explain what is happening at each stage. This helps participants stay focused.
▶ Encourage interaction between the sites.
▶ Aim for a balance of views and opinions.
▶ Try to sustain the pace and momentum, e.g. by picking up on points that might need further discussion, by inviting new points or questions.
▶ Summarise the key points of the conference.
▶ Discuss possible follow-up.
▶ Thank invited speaker(s) and all participants formally.
▶ Close the videoconference at the pre-arranged time.

After the videoconference

▶ Thank the participants informally.
▶ Give them positive feedback on their participation.
▶ Thank the technician and anyone else who may have helped off-screen. They will have played a significant part in the success of the videoconference.
▶ Invite participants to give a brief on-the-spot verbal evaluation or reaction while the experience is fresh in their minds. (This is usually volunteered with some enthusiasm!)
▶ Request brief written comments when participants have had time to reflect and assimilate the experience. Ask for comments on strengths and weaknesses, on relevance to their area of interest or study, on possibilities for follow-up. Ask for suggestions for improvement.
▶ Use the evaluation to help improve future videoconferences.

Videoconferencing etiquette

Videoconferencing connects people to people audio-visually and in real time. When this unique capability is exploited, the human element takes precedence over the technology, and a sense of social presence – of communicating with "real people" – is experienced. The following simple guidelines, based on respect for people and on an understanding of the technology, will facilitate effective communication, foster good interpersonal relations and help ensure that good learning takes place.

Eye contact: As in any interpersonal context in western society, it is important to maintain eye contact. This is done best by looking at the camera which ideally should be placed directly above the monitor showing the link site. Failure to do this can lead to disengagement of the distant participants who have the unfortunate impression that they are not the focus of your attention.

Gestures and movement: Try to keep gestures and movement to a minimum, or move and gesture slowly and smoothly. Unnecessary movement, particularly with low bandwidth, can cause some picture pixilation, and can detract from effective communication.

Listening: Good listening is important in any meaningful verbal communication. It is even more so when videoconferencing. When the person on the far site is speaking, listen right through to the end of his/her contribution. In general, it is better not to interrupt, regardless of how enthused or interested you are in what is being said. This is for technical reasons as well as for courtesy, as interruption will distort the signal. Good chairing will allow for lively debate and discussion while respecting this protocol. It is particularly important to avoid interruption when using a voice-activated system as the camera follows the speaker. Avoid rustling papers, tapping pencils, drumming fingers or making any other unnecessary noise near the microphone. Communication should always be with the far site. There should never be same site conversations or discussions.

Speaking: It goes without saying that speaking naturally, clearly and distinctly is a basic requirement for effective oral communication. Nowhere is this more so than in videoconferencing. We must also consider language issues when linking participants from different parts of the world. Even when participants share a common language, e.g. English, differences in accents and poor diction can cause difficulties and misunderstanding in communication. When videoconferencing with people for whom English is not the first language, it is important to speak slightly more slowly and more distinctly than usual and to avoid using colloquialisms. Of course, slow stilted speech is also to be avoided; it is equally detrimental to free-flowing communication. It should be stressed very strongly that local accents are not in themselves a problem in videoconferencing. Indeed, they are to be welcomed as part of the enrichment of cultural diversity. When we – and our partners – speak clearly, effective communication takes place, enlivened by our different accents! Remember that videoconferencing is a visual medium. Use body language e.g. a smile, a nod, to convey your reactions. Remember too that negative body language, e.g. bored expression, grimaces, slumped position, can all be seen clearly.

Dress code: Adherence to a simple dress code will enable the technology to function smoothly. Avoid prints, stripes, checks, plaids, shiny jewellery. These are very distracting to the camera. Wear solid colours. Blue and green work well, red less so.

CONCLUSION

Videoconferencing can enrich and extend the learning experiences available in the traditional classroom. It largely overcomes the barriers to learning imposed by time, distance, expense and the limitations of human energy. It has the potential to connect learners of all ages and abilities, audiovisually and in real time, to colleagues, experts, and other communities and experiences in a virtual but meaningful interactive way that can enhance their learning and enrich their lives. The technology is now robust and increasingly affordable, and with the availability of higher bandwidth videoconferencing has become a realistic option for the classroom. The challenge facing schools now is no longer about the videoconferencing technology, but about using it to transform the learning environment.

It is now increasingly accepted by educators that 21st century education needs to focus on authentic learning situations in order to close the gap between the real world and the world of school, and to engage the new generation of learners who are growing up in a fast and constantly changing digital world. Videoconferencing, with its potential for bringing the outside world into the classroom and for interactive knowledge building, obviously has a major role to play in addressing these issues. Not only can it help provide the hard benefits of extending and enriching the curriculum, supporting inter-school collaborative work and professional development of teachers; it also fosters the development of the "portable" and "soft" skills required by the work place. The case for integrating this technology into the school curriculum is becoming increasingly stronger. Studies have shown, however, that the effectiveness of videoconferencing in schools depends less on the technology itself than on the way the teacher uses it and the teacher's attitude toward it. In the final analysis, it is the creative use of videoconferencing by enthusiastic teachers who are sensitive to the unique capabilities of the technology that makes the real difference. These teachers exploit its potential for enriching, expanding and ultimately transforming the learning environment in ways that we are only beginning to realise. My hope is that the good practice stories of such teachers, together with the practical guidance offered in these pages, will encourage and motivate others to follow suit and to discover even more effective and successful ways of using videoconferencing to meet the needs of all learners and to bring authentic learning to life in schools.

Appendices

Appendix A
Bibliography and Online Resources

Bibliography

Arnold,   T., Cayley, S., & Griffith, M. (2004). *Video conferencing in the classroom: Communications technology across the curriculum.* Devon: Devon County Council.

Comber,   C., Lawson, T., Gage, J., Cullum-Hanshaw, A., & Allen, T. (2004). *Report for schools of the DfES video conferencing in the classroom project.* Available at http://www.becta.org.uk/page_documents/research/video_conferencing_report_may04.pdf

Cole,   C., Ray, K., & Zanetis, J. (2004). *Videoconferencing for K-12 classrooms.* Eugene, OR: International Society for Technology in Education.

Newman,   D.L., Falco, L., & Silverman, S. (Eds.) (2008). *Videoconferencing technology in K-12 instruction: Best practices and trends.* Hershey, PA: Idea Publishing Group.

Online Resources (active at the time of writing)

http://dl.remc11.k12.mi.us/fieldtripsites/FMPro?-DB=fieldtripsites&-Format=providerlist.htm&-Error=search_error.htm&-Op=&ShortDescription=a&-SortField=SiteName&-Max=300&-Find
An outstanding resource. It gives a list of 226 providers – mainly US-based, but also some excellent ones from the UK, Spain and Canada. A direct link to the site with an overview of the programme is provided in each case. Look at Shakespeare's Globe Theatre as an example. If you have time to visit only one list of content providers, make it this one!

http://www.twice.cc/
A totally comprehensive site for videoconferencing in the primary and post-primary sectors, regularly updated, containing factual information, ideas for projects, and suggestions for finding contacts. It also offers lists of content providers.

http://www.janetcollaborate.ac.uk
Lists collaboration opportunities.

http://education.nasa.gov/home/index.html
NASA education site. Provides information on available primary and post-primary programmes, many of which are free.

http://education.nasa.gov/edprograms/stdprograms/index.html
Very comprehensive information on materials and resources associated with NASA programmes.

http://www.nasa.gov/centers/glenn/education/DigitalLearningNetwork_GRC.html
Information about NASA's Digital Learning Network which offers video-conferencing or webcasting at no charge, providing interactive educational experiences to students and educators around the world.

http://www.nassauboces.org/cit/vls/lectora/vc/index.html
A free introductory tutorial on videoconferencing.

http://www.wmnet.org.uk/vc/
Fun but practical interactive introduction to videoconferencing; highly recommended.

http://multiclass.e2bn.net/advice/index.php
Useful site; very comprehensive. (Dark background not conducive to easy reading!)

http://www.global-leap.org.uk/
Very informative, wide ranging and classroom-friendly; offers introductory

video, ongoing guidance and directory of users; annual subscription required.

http://www.teachers.ash.org.au/npressnell/ict/yhgfl.htm
A Look at the Future – a very interesting perspective.

http://motivate.maths.org/
Videoconferencing for Maths, motivation and cross-curricular themes.

http://www.shambles.net/pages/staff/VideoConf/
Lists range of videoconferencing-related education sites.

http://www.educationworld.com/a_issues/chat/chat127-2.shtm
A "second look at videoconferencing" – interview with author of *Videoconferencing for K-12 classroom.*

http://cte.umdnj.edu/technology_corner/tech_itv_teleconferencing.cfm
Excellent resource with links to other helpful sources; covers a range of videoconferencing-related issues from perspective of classroom use. (Note: The Pacific Bell links are now inactive.)

http://www.d261.k12.id.us/VCing/classroom/planning.htm
Teachers' Digital Handbook – very useful hyperlinks dealing with a range of videoconferencing-related issues from technical details to implementation strategies. It also provides tutorials, but these relate mainly to the PictureTel system.

http://www.virtual-field-trips.com/
Lists a wide range of virtual field trips. Worth exploring.

APPENDIX B
Matrix for Lesson Planning and Evaluation; Sample Videoconferencing Lesson Plans

MATRIX					
Why? When? What?	How?	Materials	Peripheral Technologies	Timeline	Evaluation
Curriculum relevance? Stage in unit of study? Learning objectives?	Preparation? Delivery methods?	Visual aids? Handouts? Worksheets? Other?	Document camera? VCR for sharing videos? Whiteboard? Computers for PPT? Other?	Duration of each segment?	Evaluation: Predicted learning outcomes? Unexpected learning outcomes? "Soft" skills? Satisfaction with technology? NB. Need for multiple perspectives – pupils (at all sites), teachers/ facilitators, external content providers, technical support personnel.

* The matrix could also serve as the basis of the evaluation of the videoconference-mediated lesson by teachers and content providers. (See Appendix C).

Sample Lesson Plan 1

Sample Lesson Plan 1 is based on Case Study 2 – Geography and Biology lesson from a professional external content provider.

Why? When? What?
- ▶ Curriculum relevance: KS 4 Geography and Biology
- ▶ Appropriate stage in learning unit: at early stage, following introductory class-based lessons
- ▶ Learning Objectives: To enrich the Geography and Biology curricula by comparing river systems in two countries, enhancing understanding of coastal erosion, deepening understanding of the differences between aquatic species and how they react with their habitat

How?
- ▶ Preparation: Internet research as advised by distant teachers/content provider; completing preparation worksheets sent by the content provider; practice videoconferences to promote pupil confidence and communication skills
- ▶ Method of delivery by agreement between class teacher and content provider/distant teachers: virtual tour with short information input by distant teachers; question and answer sessions; group activities; interactive discussions between pupils, and between pupils and teacher; pupil presentation

Materials (sent in advance by external provider)
- ▶ Worksheets
- ▶ Surgical gloves
- ▶ Maps (provided by school)

Peripheral technologies
- ▶ Document camera (near site)
- ▶ Model of estuary (far site)
- ▶ Flip chart (near site)

Timeline

- ▶ Introduction – social interaction to establish rapport between pupils and distant teacher (5 minutes)
- ▶ Brief virtual tour of Hudson River Estuary (15 minutes)
- ▶ Demonstration of model of estuary at far site and brief input on variables affecting erosion – with question and answer session (5 minutes)
- ▶ Using worksheets, pupils work in groups on devising strategies to minimise erosion (5 minutes)
- ▶ Under direction from pupils, distant teacher tests pupils' strategies on model and discusses outcomes with pupils (5 minutes)
- ▶ Surgical glove activity to enhance understanding of aquatic species (5 minutes)
- ▶ Interactive discussion between pupils and teacher (5 minutes)
- ▶ Using document camera, maps and flip chart, pupils present study of local estuary (5 minutes)
- ▶ Comments and questions from distant teacher with pupil responses (5 minutes)
- ▶ Thanks, arrangements for follow up work and wrap up (5 minutes)

Duration of distant lesson – 1 hour

Evaluation: Following the lesson, the class teacher asks for oral feedback from participants and facilitators and arranges for written evaluation from pupils, distant teacher, technical support person.

Sample Lesson Plan 2

Sample Lesson Plan 2 is based on Case Study 7 – access to US politician.

Why? When? What?

▶ Curriculum relevance: selected option on A level Politics syllabus

▶ Appropriate stage: near end of class-based unit of study to ensure solid knowledge foundation and awareness of areas needing further clarification. These would form the basis of the prepared questions for the experts.

▶ Lesson objectives: to deepen local pupils' knowledge and understanding of US constitution (part of their A level curriculum), and US pupils' knowledge and understanding of the British constitution and the NI situation through live access to primary sources; to expand pupils' horizons by introducing them to real-time distant collaborative learning using videoconferencing

How?

▶ Preparation: liaising with all schools involved to prepare a range of questions; refining questions; selecting inter-school panel of pupils; allocating questions; practice videoconferences to promote pupil confidence and communication skills

▶ Methods of delivery: brief presentations by experts; pupil panel question and answer session with experts; cross-site student panel discussions; open discussion

Materials

▶ Written questions

▶ Photos of schools

Peripheral technologies

▶ Document camera

▶ Large screen projector

▶ Radio microphone

Timeline

- Schools link-up; social interaction; free discussion; display photos of school and local area on document camera (10 minutes)
- Link-up with Congressman in House of Representatives; introductions -including expert on British constitution present at local site (5 minutes)
- Short presentation from Congressman – overview of his work and responsibilities (5 minutes)
- Question and answer session: panel of four local pupils alternates with US pupils to ask prepared questions about US constitution (15 minutes)
- Congressman and local expert compare and contrast British and US constitutions (10 minutes)
- Pupil panels respond to discussion (5 minutes)
- Questions from US pupils on NI situation; responses from local expert and local pupil panel (10 minutes)
- Open discussion on NI situation using radio microphone to include members of the audience at both sites (10 minutes)
- Thanks, arrangements for follow-up between schools and with Congressman's office (5 minutes)

Duration of lesson – 75 minutes.

Evaluation: Following the lesson the class teacher asks for oral feedback from student participants, teachers and facilitators and arranges for written evaluation from students, experts, teachers and technical support personnel.

Appendix C
Sample Evaluation Form for Pupils

To indicate the level of your agreement with statements 1-12, please circle one number in the range 1-4, according to the following indicators:

1 STRONGLY DISAGREE	3 AGREE
2 DISAGREE	4 STRONGLY AGREE

1. I enjoyed the overall videoconferencing experience.

    1   2   3   4

2. I now have a better understanding of the topic we were studying.

    1   2   3   4

3. I feel more motivated to continue my study of the topic.

    1   2   3   4

4. I feel more confident now about learning with videoconferencing.

    1   2   3   4

5. I feel more confident now about working as part of a virtual team.

    1   2   3   4

6. The videoconferencing technology worked well.

    1   2   3   4

7. I was able to forget about the technology.

    1   2   3   4

8. I felt I was dealing with real people.

      1   2   3   4

9. I felt actively involved in the experience.

      1   2   3   4

10. The length of the videoconference was just right.

      1   2   3   4

11. There was plenty of variety in the videoconference.

      1   2   3   4

12. I would like to do videoconferencing again.

      1   2   3   4

To help us improve the experience of learning through videoconferencing, please

- indicate any areas that you were not happy with

- suggest ways in which these could be improved

- add any other comments

Note: Evaluation for teachers and content providers could be based on the matrix in Appendix B.

APPENDIX D
Glossary of common videoconferencing-related terms

Application
How you make use of a technology
Also commonly used to denote computer software.

Asynchronous communication
Communication that does not occur in real time. Email and discussion board communications are examples of this.

Bandwidth
The capacity of a link or services to carry data, measured in bits per second (bps), thousands of bits per second (kbps) or millions of bits per second (mpbs). Bandwidth capacity determines the amount of data – video, audio, or text – that can be transmitted through network channels in a given amount of time.

Bridge
Also known as Multipoint Conferencing Units (MCU); connects three or more videoconference sites.

Broadband
Refers to the capacity of a link or communications circuit.

Camera pre-sets
Pre-selected camera sets or angles programmed into a videoconferencing system to allow anyone speaking to be more quickly identified.

Content provider
A professional or informal agency that provides educational content to schools using videoconferencing.

Dedicated videoconferencing systems
Stand-alone units suitable for use with a range of user sizes – one-to one, small groups, large groups.

Desktop videoconferencing
Videoconferencing using a computer or videophone; generally used for one-to-one or small group communication.

Digital learners
Also known as the net generation – young people who have grown up in a technology-saturated world which has shaped their learning needs and styles.

Distance education
Also known as distance learning or e-learning – learning events where the participants are separated by physical space and/or time, and technology is used to bridge the gap.

Document camera
Also called a visualiser, a camera mounted above a flat surface, used to show pictures, maps, posters, documents or physical objects.

Echo cancellation
Sometimes the microphone at the far site picks up your voice after you speak and plays it back to you causing an echo. An echo cancellation feature may be built into the system to eliminate this.

End-users
The participants at each site in a videoconference.

Facilitator
The person physically present at the far site who assists pupils during a videoconference where the teacher/expert is accessed virtually

Far site
Also known as link site, far-end site or distant/remote site. This refers to the distant videoconferencing system to which you are linked.

Firewall
A security device to control data passing through a network and to prevent unauthorised access to the network.

Interactive whiteboard
White board with electronic sensors on surface material. When a computer image is displayed onto the whiteboard, the computer can be controlled from the board using the finger or a special pen. White-boarding can enable collaborative work to take place.

IP
Internet Protocol: the standard for addressing devices and transmitting data between devices on a network.

IP Videoconferencing
Conferencing between local area networks (LAN) or wide area networks (WAN) and between networks. IP calls are cost-free. Picture and audio quality may be affected by traffic on the network.

ISDN
Integrated Services Digital Network: telephone lines allowing faster data transfer rates than standard analogue lines; generally reliable for videoconferencing use, but calls can be expensive.

Mute
Switching off the microphone so that sound from one site cannot be picked up at the other; helps improve audio quality when someone at the far site is speaking.

Peripheral technology/hardware
Also known as external devices – pieces of equipment such as VCRs/DVDs, electronic whiteboard, document cameras that add features to a videoconferencing system but are not integral to it.

Synchronous communication
Two-way "live" communication (i.e. in real time).

Streaming

The delivery of audio and video across the internet; this can then be accessed via a computer. Videoconferences can be streamed live, opening up the conference to more participants who can watch it live and respond via other media. Streaming can also be used for archiving purposes.

Transparent technology

Technology that does not get in the way of learning; it functions so smoothly that participants become unaware of it and focus on the learning event.

Virtual classroom

A virtual learning environment where teachers and pupils are physically separated and technology is used to enable communication. Uniquely, videoconferencing replicates the physical classroom by enabling audiovisual communication in real time, thus fostering relationships and facilitating interactive learning.

Virtual Classroom

This is a desktop collaboration suite with audio and video conferencing, messaging and whiteboard capabilities. It operates using 'virtual rooms', which participants enter to join a session.

Virtual field trip

A real time trip made possible by videoconferencing which allows the participants to interact audiovisually in a live event with remotely located field trip hosts and peers.

Voice activated

Cameras can be voice activated to focus automatically on the person speaking during a videoconference.

Appendix E
C2k Managed Videoconferencing Service

C2k provides a video communications service to all schools in Northern Ireland. A desktop videoconferencing solution, known as Virtual Classroom, is available to all schools. A catalogue service is also available for schools who wish to purchase dedicated Tandberg videoconferencing units and peripheral hardware.

C2k has invested substantially in its data centre infrastructure to allow successful videoconferencing to take place between schools in Northern Ireland and other participants throughout the world. A scheduling facility for both desktop and dedicated videoconferencing solutions is available to all users, giving the schools independence to control their own videoconferencing sessions.

C2k has connected to the JANET network – the UK's education and research network. This allows schools in Northern Ireland to avail of the JANET videoconferencing services and of services offered by content providers which are registered with JANET.

For more information regarding the C2k Video Communications Services, please go to www.c2kexchange.net (from within school network) or https://www.c2kexchange.net (from outside school network).